CENTRE FOR THE STUDY OF ISLAM AND OTHER FAITHS

CSIOF Bulletin

Issue No. 3
November 2010

CSIOF Bulletin
ISSN 1836-3490
© 2010 Bible College of Victoria. All rights reserved

Editor
Peter Riddell

Assistant Editor
Kathryn Simon

Production
Ho-yuin Chan

Cover Design
Philip Brookes

Publishing Services
Deror Books

Centre for the Study of Islam and Other Faiths
Bible College of Victoria
PO Box 380, 71-81 Albert Hill Rd, Lilydale Vic 3140, Australia.
Ph: 0011 +61 3 9735 0011, Fax: 0011 +61 3 9735 0721
csiof@bcv.vic.edu.au, www.bcv.vic.edu.au

People involved in the field of Muslim-Christian relations are welcome to submit related items to the Editor for consideration for publishing in the CSIOF Bulletin.

Opinions and conclusions published in the CSIOF Bulletin are those of the authors and do not necessarily represent the views of the Editor or the CSIOF. The Bulletin is purely an information medium, to inform interested parties of religious trends, discussions and debates. The Bulletin does not intend in any way to actively promote hatred of any religion or its followers.

EDITORIAL	3
FEATURES	4
Islam: Unity in Diversity 1	5
Islam: Unity in Diversity 2	13
Muslim Scholars Address the Hadith	21
Making of a Missionary: the Da'iyya	30
Australia Looks Towards Edinburgh 2010	41
Christian Mission Among Other Faiths	44
Contextual Mission: An Australian Perspective	50
COMMUNIQUÉS	57
Graduate Seminar in Theology in Stuttgart	57
The Islamic Republic of Britain? A Personal Odyssey	58
REVIEWS	63
The Story of the Qur'an	63
The Banquet: A Reading of the Fifth Sura of the Qur'an	66
Approaches to the Qur'an in Contemporary Indonesia	68
Islamic Legal Thought in Modern Indonesia	71
God's Battalions	73
World of the Spirits	76
The Wedding Song	81
The Third Choice	85
A God who Hates	87
The World Turned Upside Down	89
Another Attack on the Reliability of the Bible	92
CSIOF NEWS AND ACTIVITIES	97
Postgraduate Research Seminars on Islam 2010	100

Editorial

The first two features in this latest issue of the *CSIOF Bulletin* provide different angles on the question of unity and diversity within the world of Islam, considering the elements of "glue" that bind the rich variety across the Islamic world.

The remaining features present papers delivered at two very different conferences. On 4 August 2010 an inter-institutional Day Conference was held at the Australian Catholic University in Melbourne, bringing together doctoral researchers from ACU, Monash University and the CSIOF. The feature articles on the Hadith and the Da'iyya were presented as papers by CSIOF researchers at that event.

On 2-3 October 2009, a conference was held in Melbourne to mark the centenary of the great 1910 Edinburgh missions conference, and to anticipate a centenary celebration planned for Edinburgh in June 2010. The Melbourne gathering is described in my own brief contribution, followed by the two plenary addresses that were given on 3 October 2010.

Two communiqués follow, providing windows into Christian-Muslim issues in Germany and Britain. Then comes a series of reviews of books and films, covering wide-ranging topics and locations of relevance to the study of Islam. This issue of the *Bulletin* concludes with a summary of news and activities from the CSIOF over the last twelve months.

This *Bulletin* issue predominantly considers the study of Islam and Christian-Muslim relations. Normally, the *Bulletin* will also include material relevant to other world religions, especially Judaism, Hinduism and Buddhism. Readers with an interest in these other faiths are invited to submit material for possible inclusion in future issues of the *Bulletin*.

The material contained in this issue reflects a range of Christian viewpoints vis-à-vis the study of other religions. This is appropriate, given the rich tapestry of Christian thought on this subject and the great diversity among Muslims. We will seek to maintain such a breadth of views in future issues of the *Bulletin*.

We do hope you enjoy reading the wealth of material presented in the following pages.

Peter Riddell

Islam: Unity in Diversity

Peter Johnstone

Islam as a world faith appears integrated and all encompassing, applying to all areas of life; theological, political, social and cultural. However, this does not mean that it is monochromatic, and there are many shades and hues in both beliefs and praxis. In reality, its 1.3 billion adherents do not agree in many areas, and there is a plurality of Islamic expressions that have adapted to local cultures and personal interpretation. While there is an Islamic overlay, there is a degree of syncretism that operates beneath the surface of the external cultural form. Nevertheless, given this great diversity, what factors actually do hold it together as a world faith?

In its first draft, this paper sought to identify factors that fell under the four main areas mentioned above, that is, theological, political, social and cultural. Yet, despite attempts to classify according to this schema, the interconnectedness of each factor militated against such a simplistic categorization. Several factors could quite justifiably be placed under more than one topic heading. Therefore, this constructionist methodology was abandoned, and the factors are now simply identified in the following discussion by highlighting them in bold italics. For stylistic reasons, because I wished to affirm their interconnectedness, I chose not to use paragraph headings.

Factors

The first factor would seemingly be a pure theological one. That is, the majority of Muslim interpreters (both cleric and lay) use a *Non-Critical Hermeneutic* when it comes to the Qur'an, Hadith and Sirat al-Nabi. [1] While there are isolated examples of a few academics that are prepared to risk 'critical' revisionist methodologies, the majority are content to affirm that Muhammad is the last and most pre-eminent of a long line of prophetic witnesses dating back to Adam.[2] Allah's authoritative revelations, (as revealed to Muhammad), and Muhammad's Sunnah, (as popularly

---

[1] This is affirmed by Riaz Hassan research involving 6390 Muslim respondents from seven countries in South-East Asia, South Asia, Central Asia, and the Middle East. Riaz Hassan. *Inside Muslim Minds* (Melbourne: Melbourne University Press, 2008).

[2] *Sahih Muslim* Book 4 Hadith No. 1062.

understood), are uncritically accepted by the vast majority of adherents.

Because of this, when verses such as Surat 9:33 & 48:28 are read they are readily accepted as absolute Truth. These Qur'anic verses affirm the strong belief in the superiority of Islam over other faith and belief systems. There is no questioning on the historicity of these and other verses contained in the Qur'an and Hadith. While there are volumes of legal interpretations based on these primary documents, those discussions are constrained by the boundaries imposed by these presuppositions.[3]

The Qur'an and Hadith have not gone through the same rigorous criticism that assailed Biblical scholarship in the 18th and 19th centuries. If they did, the universalistic claims held by the majority of Muslims, "that Islam is the ultimate divine revelation, valid for all people regardless of time and space"[4], would be open to revision.[5]

When the Covenant of Medina of 622 A.D. was signed it created a new community of believers (Ummah), where familial or tribal affiliations were subjugated to a religious one. It birthed *The 'Idea' of the Islamic Ummah,* which is a popular and unifying concept held by many adherents. Its power lies in its ambiguity and generality. "Through much of Islamic history, difficulties of mass travel and communication nurtured the myth of 'one religion, one culture' and a sense of belonging to a universal Ummah."[6] A corollary to this concept of Ummah is that of *Dar al Harb* (House of War), and *Dar al Islam* (House of Peace). Though originally posited by the respected jurist Abu Hanifa (d. 148 A.H.), at a time when the Umayyad Caliphate had made vast military gains in neighbouring countries, this dichotomy has been utilized as a rallying point for the militaristic expansion of Islamic forces throughout history.[7]

---

[3] In many ways this is similar to Catholic Scholasticism that affected the medieval church from 1100-1500 A.D.

[4] Bassam Tibi, Islam between Culture and Politics (2nd ed.; Hampshire: Palgave Macmillian Ltd, 2005), 91.

[5] This non-critical hermeneutic can also overflow into other areas, particularly historiographical method and politics, and has at times been utilised to manipulate whole populations towards a particular course of action, often with disastrous consequences.

[6] Riaz Hassan, *Inside Muslim Minds* (Melbourne: Melbourne University Press, 2008), 6.

[7] Following the 1989 Sudanese coup d'état by Brigadier Omar al-Bashir the ongoing civil war with the South intensified – the confrontation being described using the conceptual terms *Dar al Harb* and *Dar al Islam*.

Historical antecedents are important in Islam; the memory of the former greatness of past Islamic empires often writ large upon both individual and the collective psyche of believers. There is a strong desire to return to Islam's former glory (as popularly understood) to once again be the dominant political, economic and religious force across the world.

The flip side to this collectivist yearning is *A Reaction against Western Hegemony* in international affairs, where the United States is perceived as the main enemy. The horrors of the Second World War awakened the 'sleeping giant' from its neutrality and isolationist policies to become the dominant player in world politics. Many Muslim states, transnational groups and individual adherents, are prepared to put aside individual differences to unite against this common 'foe'. It is definitely a case of, 'The enemy of my enemy is my friend'. The US influence as the world's police officer is deeply resented in many Muslim countries, as is the negative aspects of western culture that is pervading a globalized world. "Western hegemony is viewed by orthodox Muslims as well as by fundamentalists as a situation that came about at the expense of Islam." (Tibi 2005: 91) To further complicate the issue, US economic sanctions and military action against so-called 'rogue' Islamic states have polarised public opinion in Muslim lands, only deepening the longing for a return to former days when Islam was '*The*' world power of old.

As a result, there are huge social and political pressures in Islamic countries to reject western influences and remain part of the Islamic collective.[8] Changing religion (or having a non-normative version of Islam) is seen as a rejection of the values of the community, and, in the case where religious belief is constitutionally mandated, a treasonous act against the state punishable by death.[9]

The end of World War One, and resultant demise of the Ottoman Empire, ushered in a turbulent period of nationalization in the lands of the former Caliphate, and those under the control of the colonial

---

[8] On 25th September 1969 the Organisation of the Islamic Conference was formed. It now has 57 member states who are signatories to their Charter with one of the agreed articles to enhance and consolidate the bonds of fraternity and solidarity among the Member States. Information from Organization of The Islamic Conference Website http://www.oic-oci.org/page_detail.asp?p_id=52.

[9] Mahmoud Muhammad Taha was executed in 1985 by the Northern Sudan government for holding to aberrant views about the legitimacy of revelations received by Muhammad after his flight to Medina in 622 A.D.

powers. In the years immediately following the end of World War Two this shift of power continued with patriotic fervour, as many former colonies became sovereign states governed by their own peoples. The 1960 United Nations Declaration of the Ending of Colonialism completed the move, and by the middle of that decade, many of the former colonial countries had experimented with their own governments. By and large, these were based on political systems adapted from their former colonial masters. Unfortunately, for the vast majority of these countries, these grand attempts were not successful. Poor economic performance, a decline in living standards, nepotism and corruption were rife. Widespread dissatisfaction became frustration, which often boiled over into violent sedition, as one coup d'état followed another. This *Post-colonial Collapse of Nation States,* in countries where Muslims were the majority, led to the *Politicisation of Islam,* where there was a natural movement towards installing Islamic governments. The rationale was that previous governments had failed because they were not following Islamic principles and Shari 'a. However, in contrast to grander times, when Islamic empires were ruled under the Caliphate and his viziers, Islam had now been politicized within the defined borders of sovereign states, with nationalistic identities, and authoritative rulers. Thus Islam became a tool for political control. And, as the Moroccan Islamist leader Nadia Yassin once said,

> "If I go into the streets and I call people to come with me to a demonstration, and I talk to them about Che Guevara and Lenin, nobody will go out. But if I start talking about Muhammad, and Ali and Aisha and all the prophets of Islam, they will follow me."[10]

This nationalistic movement was aided because Muslim communities have generally been *collectivist societies,* and not individualist in orientation. Individual faith decisions were not made in isolation from the local community which acted to strongly normalise thinking, decisions, and behaviour along accepted societal patterns. If a person was born to a Muslim family, in a majority Muslim country, their religious identity was often influenced by multiple layers within a homogeneous community that upheld similar beliefs, values and rituals.

---

[10] George Packer, 'The Moderate Martyr: a radically peaceful vision of Islam' in *The New Yorker* http://www.newyorker.com/archive/2006/09/11/060911fa_fact1?currentPage=all#ixzz0mqzHT27f (11 Sept, 2006).

In current days, the ease of personal mobility, access to worldwide media, and communication has made it possible for individuals to go beyond their traditional community identity, and engage in multiple communities that are not geographically isolated. As a result, it is now possible for an individual to hold 'multiple' identities.

From a sociological perspective, it is possible for an individual to assert a particular religious identity at one point, and yet, concurrently affirm beliefs and practices that would be seen as incongruent to such a belief, and indicate quite a different identity. *The Non-Specificity of the Term Muslim* makes it difficult to define the essential characteristics necessary to categorise it into a 'bounded set'[11]. Instead there is actually a *Strong Case for Multiple Identities* being affirmed. Therefore, it is perhaps more helpful to consider the multiple relationship model of 'fuzzy sets' being used to describe identity, where degrees of inclusion can be affirmed, with the term 'Muslim' being dependant on the strength of relationship that the individual agrees to. This is pertinent to our discussion as there is a wide secularizing movement (particularly in Western countries) where a Muslim identity is just one of several that a person could affirm depending on their context, and community they are relating to at the time.

Against this secularizing movement, many Muslims living as minorities actually resist integration into their new adopted society, and instead, reaffirm their home community's adherence to Islam – even at times becoming more 'religious' than they would be in those countries. Alternatively, the individual may hold to traditional symbols, but will seek to reinterpret those symbols to give personal identity and make sense of their new situation. (Rippin 2005: 258)

Therefore, when an individual affirms that 'I am a Muslim', one needs to identify which community (or communities, if any) inform that self-designation: i.e. what are they actually affirming? Is it their

---

[11] Just saying the 'shahada' in front of witnesses does not make one a 'Muslim'. There are other essential elements that need to be included. However, there is wide dispute as to what these essential elements should include. For example, current day Islamists are quick to denounce individuals (or whole communities) as non-Islamic that do not hold to their particular jihadist interpretations. Alternatively, many moderate Muslims are quick to criticize the Islamists as standing outside the realm of the faithful because of their literalistic interpretation of the Qur'an and willingness to utilize violence and terror as a legitimate means of propagating Islam. The recent fatwa issued by Shaykh-ul-Islam Dr Muhammad Tahir-ul-Qadri, the founding leader and patron-in-chief of Minhaj-ul-Quran International, is an example of this.
See video presentation of this: http://www.youtube.com/watch?v=KNDanFjzHek.

part of the worldwide community of believers (the Ummah); or their nationalistic or tribal identity[12]; or their theological or sectarian affiliations; or their familial religious association; or simply an individual designation, that is "ever personal and flexible" (Rippin 2005: 276); or a combination of all of them? To a non-informed outsider, the self designation of a person as 'Muslim' evokes *an image of unity* and participation with a worldwide faith that overstates the complexity of the real situation.

Nonetheless, assisting this unifying image is the normalizing factor of *Strong External Similarities in Ritual Worship and Practice*, for the vast majority of Muslims. The formal prayer ritual, often imbedded into their psyche from an early age, continues to be reinforced by their respective communities, particularly where Islam, be it Sunni or Shi'a, is the dominant religion. While there may be sectarian or regional variations, having a common sacred form that is repeated in unison with a group of individuals at prescribed times gives the sense of being part of something far bigger than just that local expression.

The Ramadan fast is also a strong unifying ritual, where in majority countries the whole community will change its diurnal practices, and faith is often reinvigorated. In countries where Muslims are the minority, it helps to achieve a sense of corporate identity. Here, the fast is often broken with other adherents, and the significant feast days are communally celebrated with joyous enthusiasm.

The Hajj is another major ritual which promotes a unified image of Islam. [13] A recent Harvard University study found, "that participation in the Hajj increases observance of global Islamic practices such as prayer and fasting. It increases belief in equality and harmony among ethnic groups and Islamic sects..."[14] Through these external rituals, the believer, (and those looking in from outside), is left with a strong subliminal *image* of a unified faith.

---

[12] An example of this is that of Kazakhstan. Riaz Hassan suggests, "that all Kazaks identified Islam as part of their ethnic and linguistic heritage. Their 'Muslim-ness' was more cultural than religious"- Riaz Hassan, *Inside Muslim Minds* (Melbourne: Melbourne University Press, 2008), 13.

[13] Even though many Muslims find the control by the Saudi government somewhat perplexing, particularly when they seek to limit attendance of certain groups of Muslims as happened during the period of the Iran –Iraq war. Andrew Rippin, *Muslims: Their Religious Beliefs and Practices* (London: Routledge, 2005, 3rd ed.), 269.

[14] Sayedeh Kasmai-Nazeran, 'A Peace Building Tool for Muslims: The Hajj' in *Islamic Insights* http://www.islamicinsights.com/religion/religion/a-peacebuilding-tool-for-muslims-hajj.html (22 June, 2008).

Conclusion

Some factors I have mentioned have an enduring quality about them and are not affected by the passage of time; others are more contemporary and context-specific. The *Non-Critical Hermeneutic,* which controls the theological enterprise, is being challenged, albeit by a very few revisionist scholars. *The 'Idea' of the Islamic Ummah,* and its corollary, the division of the world into *Dar al Harb & Dar al Islam* are conceptual tools which support the Universalist notion that Islam is truly a world religion, valid for all peoples, at all times and places. *The Reality of Western Hegemony* thwarts this Universalistic modality and unites Islamic groups that would not normally be so cooperative. The 20th Century *Post-Colonial Collapse of Nation States leading to a Politicization of Islam* means that Islam is now imbedded in the structure of sovereign nation states that exert their political and religious agendas on the world scene. In majority countries, this nationalism has been assisted by the sociological phenomenon that *Muslim communities are generally collectivist societies that* hold to common beliefs, values and religious identity. However, within a globalized world it is now possible for an individual to accommodate *Multiple Identities* one which, (depending on the circumstances and community of affiliation), could be Islamic or not. The *Non-Specificity of the Term Muslim* complicates exactly who is an adherent to this world religion. *Strong External Similarities in Ritual Worship and Practice,* particularly in prayer, the Ramadan fast, and the Hajj, do give the individual a sense of belonging to a greater whole, and therefore ameliorates this sense of particularization.

The best material analogy for Islam is that of a multifaceted 'Rubik's Cube', whereby its essential unity is fragmented by different facets that can twist and turn in relationship to one another. It is a world faith, but a fragmented one. The challenge for the Islamic faith in the 21st Century will be whether it can control the centrifugal forces that seek to destroy its unifying factors. Viewed from different perspectives these factors either come to the forefront or subside to the background, but they all make a contribution in holding Islam together as a world faith.

Bibliography

Ayoob, Mohammed, *The Many Faces of Political Islam - Religion and Politics in Muslim World* (Ann Arbour: The University of Michigan Press, 2008).

Hassan, Riaz, *Inside Muslim Minds* (Melbourne: Melbourne University Press, 2008).

Karsh, Efraim. *Islamic Imperialism: A history* (New Haven: Yale University Press, 2007).

Kasmai-Nazeran, Sayedeh. 'A Peace Building Tool for Muslims: The Hajj' in *Islamic Insights*, http://www.islamicinsights.com/religion/religion/a-peacebuilding-tool-for-muslims-hajj.html (22 June, 2008).

Lapidus, Ira M. *A History of Islamic Societies* (Cambridge: Cambridge University Press, 2002).

Muhammad Tahir ul Qadri, 'Fatwa on Suicide Bombings and Terrorism' http://www.youtube.com/watch?v=KNDanFjzHek (2 March 2010).

Packer, George. 'The Moderate Martyr: a radically peaceful vision of Islam' in *The New Yorker* http://www.newyorker.com/archive/2006/09/11/060911fa_fact1?currentPage=all#ixzz0mqzHT27f (11 Sept 2006).

Rippin, Andrew. *Muslims: Their Religious Beliefs and Practices* (London: Routledge, 2005, 3rd ed.).

Stille Alexander. 'Radical New Views of Islam and the Origins of the Koran' http://www.rim.org/muslim/qurancrit.htm (2 March 2002).

Tibi, Bassam, *Islam between Culture and Politics* (2nd ed.; Hampshire: Palgave Macmillian Ltd, 2005).

Websites Consulted:

www.minhaj.org

www.oic-oci.org

www.quran.com

Islam: Unity in Diversity

Dr John Kingsbury

The factors holding Islam together as a world faith can be grouped in three broad categories. Firstly, there is a cluster of qualities inherent to the faith that a disinterested secular observer, or even an objective one of another religious persuasion, can deem to be 'positive'. For example, no one can deny the incredibly cohesive influence of the Prophet Muhammad's life and words. Secondly, there are a number of factors contributing to the unity of Islam, which whether understood as integral or aberrational, are viewed negatively through the eyes of those of other faiths. For example, the geographical expansion of Islam at the expense of others has endowed it with an enormous unifying strength. Thirdly, there are several factors contributing to Islamic unity from outside the faith itself that have come about through the law of unintended consequences. An oft-cited example is the rallying power of the call to remember the Crusades.

As well as examining elements within each of the three categories delineated above, this paper will also ask qualitative questions about the *degree* of unity in Islam, rather than simply assuming that the faith has held together or is holding together in any *absolute* sense. The need to acknowledge the observable unity-in-diversity of Islam, while simultaneously asking the question, 'but how well?' has been succinctly captured by Cragg's observation: '... in the circumstances of the contemporary world [albeit writing in 1956], the failure of the household of Islam to achieve any outward form of unity higher than a fragmentary nationalism need not be interpreted as implying any essential failure in the consciousness of Muslim singularity in the face of the non-Muslim world.'[15] Further, it is my intent to ask, in relation to some of the factors, whether contemporary developments pertaining to them are likely to engender a greater sense of unity or be catalytic in pulling Islam apart.

---

[15] K. Cragg, *The Call of the Minaret* (Oxford, Oneworld, 2000), 176.

In this first and largest section on 'positive' factors holding Islam together, I will discuss the significance of Muhammad, the Qur'an, and the ritual practices of the faith. While the supremacy and indivisibility of Allah is the bedrock of Islamic belief, it is the person of his Messenger, the Prophet Muhammad, who acts as the centripetal human face drawing Muslims into the heart of their faith. Muhammad is the ideal 'type' to which individual Muslims aspire, he is the exalted recipient of God's fullest and final revelations, and he is portrayed through his *sunna* as teacher extraordinaire. Rippin sums up the breadth of this charismatic figure's unifying force by saying,

'All Muslim groups in the modern world join in their veneration of Muhammad.'[16] It would be an uncharitable observer indeed who failed to acknowledge this prophet and statesman's tenacity in the face of setbacks and his single-mindedness in upholding the truth revealed to him.

It is important, however, to name two biographical aspects that may lead in time to somewhat less than '*all* Muslim groups' sharing such a high view of the Prophet. Traditional biographies, including ones by non-Muslims for a general audience, while not blatantly dishonest, skew the picture of Muhammad's life and character by omitting unpalatable and awkward details.[17] For example, the endearing and readily includable hadith about the Prophet's tender care of a cat sleeping on the sleeve of his robe[18], does not sit consistently alongside injunctions to kill infidel women, or a willingness to allow them to be killed.[19] If a fuller, 'warts and all' presentation, based on existing sources becomes available for mass consumption, then the resulting disillusionment with a fallible human being could well undermine unity. And a second biographical risk may exacerbate this. If through new scholarship, details of the Prophet's life, whether glowing or unflattering, are found to lack basis in history, then a modernist reinterpretation will have to possess remarkable rigour to ensure its subject remains a magnet of unity and lode of authority.

---

[16] A. Rippin, *Muslims: Their Religious Beliefs and Practices* (London and New York: Routledge, 2005, 3rd ed.), 200.

[17] I would include Michael Cook's biography, for example, in this category, *Muhammad* (Oxford: University Press, 1983).

[18] C. Nizamoglu, 'Cats in Islamic Culture', 2007, http://muslimheritage.com/topics/default.cfm?ArticleID=686. Cited 10 May 2010.

[19] Ibn Ishaq p.675, 676; Ibn Ishaq p.551; Abu Dawud p.4348, 4349; Ibn Ishaq p.664, 665.

Like conjoined twins, Muhammad is inseparable from the Qur'an, the 'defining point of Islamic identity.'[20] Cragg, who of all non-Muslim scholars probably gets the closest to feeling the heartbeat of Islam, senses how deeply the Qur'an provides the essence of unity in the faith across any time period and through the ages: 'As the speech of God it shares God's eternity. But its place in the interior life of Islam does not turn upon theological reasoning alone. It is established by centuries of veneration, by generations of being a people of the Book. Its familiar surahs are recited at birth and in bereavement, repeated in the crises between, and breathed in the long piety of all the generations.'[21] While a meaningful comparison of the relative importance of the Qur'anic and biblical texts for the respective faiths is extremely difficult, a case of sorts could be made for viewing the former as more inherently essential for the maintenance of unity.

Whether though, like its twin and original recipient, the Qur'an is going to *remain* as an adhesive, holding diverse groups and persuasions together is a moot point. It is not difficult to imagine the trickle of scholarship from the past 20 to 30 years that is questioning the miraculousness of the Qur'an in favour of a text with a history and seeking to remove its anti-rational elements, becoming a stream of revisionism that sweeps through Islam like an Arabian desert storm threatening the integrity of the faith. Is this an exaggeration? Rippin, who himself is at the forefront of critical analysis, asks how far the process can be taken 'without destroying Islam'.[22] And if the Qur'an's reliability and consequent authority is seen to be tenuously situated on shaky ground, then the whole corpus of Islamic literature – Hadith, legal texts, commentaries, and stories of the prophets – will prove to be a house of cards. How successful will the Qur'anic text continue to be in holding together the faith it has birthed, if Puin's assertion that 'every fifth sentence or so simply doesn't make sense', becomes the scholarly consensus?[23]

A third factor in my first grouping would seem to be much less under threat as a unifier of the Islamic faith than the preceding two. One does not have to spend long in a Muslim country to appreciate

---

[20] A. Rippin, *Muslims*, 37.

[21] K. Cragg, *The Call of the Minaret*, 186.

[22] A. Rippin, *Muslims*, 147.

[23] G. Puin in T. Lester, 'What is the Koran?' *The Atlantic Monthly* (1999), 43-56.

how much the ritual and practices of the faith define identity, provide comfort and purpose, and cement the individual into the life of the community. My way of contrasting life in Pakistan with that in a secular country like New Zealand has been to describe Islam as 'permeating every nook and cranny of daily life'. Rippin describes ritual as being very important 'both from the perspective of self-identity and for identity from the outside.'[24] It is easy for students of the religion to rattle off the 'five pillars' of Islam; it is quite another to live submerged in the daily rhythm of the calls to prayer from the minaret and to know that whether nominal or devout, these Muslims live with the constant reminders that they are part of a group that spills out across the world like ripples on a lake. Rippin, with reference to the centrality of the place of prayer, expresses this belongingness in a comparable way: '... the mosque has become ... a source of identity for the individual believers and a symbol and centre of purity for the Muslim community.'[25]

As Christians we sometimes refer disparagingly to those who are 'Sunday believers'. While unquestionably there are similarly multitudes of 'Friday Muslims', it is much more difficult for them to live within this narrow expression of faith than it is for adherents of other religions. Cragg describes Islam as a total way of life that expresses itself 'not only in the mosque but also in the market.'[26] Alongside this all-pervasiveness of Islam, it is important to recognize that the ritual practices provide an intrinsic simplicity to the faith that has great appeal. Unlike Christianity with its 'illogical' notion of grace that cannot be earned by actions, Islam's cohesiveness has been assisted by practices that symbolize the very human notion that the way to God is via the performance of righteous deeds. Accompanying this simplicity of ritual practice and detailing it and all other conceivable human actions, is Islam's holy law or Shari'a. The complexities of having to thoughtfully apply principles are removed by being able to make recourse to detailed legislation. Rippin describes the practical actions required by Islamic law as 'the most crucial and relevant discipline to the vast majority of Muslims.'[27]

---

[24] A. Rippin, *Muslims*, 257.

[25] A. Rippin, *Muslims*, 109.

[26] K. Cragg, *The Call of the Minaret*, 128.

[27] A. Rippin, *Muslims*, 87.

A second group of factors for consideration are those that have unquestionably contributed to unity or aided its definition, but ones that to a large extent have set the world of Islam over against other faiths and people. Here I will discuss the concept of *umma*, together with the nature of Islam as a religio-political phenomenon, and secondly the 'sixth pillar' of Islam, that of jihad, and the contemporary Islamist movements that espouse it.

The currently much vaunted notion of *umma* – a community or people – has its origins in a document from Muhammad's time called the 'Constitution of Medina'.[28] Apart from its initial importance in bringing together Muhammad's followers from Yathrib and Quraysh, the constitution was foundational in establishing one of the great defining marks of Islam – that what we refer to as the 'faith' is in fact a faith expressed within a definable *political* entity. Notwithstanding Cragg's comment above that Islam has failed to achieve any meaningful form of outward unity[29], the intangible 'spirit' of *umma* has been extraordinarily successful in creating a sense of oneness, or perhaps more accurately a sense of historical continuity and permanence. Even in the face of demonstrable and profound disunity (witness the Iran-Iraq war 1980-1988, or the incessant Sunni-Shi'ite strife in Pakistan, or the Taliban's killing of fellow Muslims) the *notion* alone of *umma* has contributed significantly to, or is the embodiment of, 'the consciousness of Muslim singularity.'[30]

Further, the importance of the *umma* in holding Islam together as a world faith lies not only in the fact of group solidarity, but also in the fact that the group is defined in contradistinction to other entities. The *dar al-Islam*, the House of Islam, is pitted against the *dar al-harb*, the House or territory of war that is yet to be brought into submission to God. This sense of mission or destiny in relation to the 'other' is a constant that has the capacity to absorb the fractiousness within the *dar al-Islam* itself. An issue though for Muslims and their unity, and one which waxes and wanes with the vagaries of history, is the question of how Islam can be truly and fully expressed when it finds itself not in the political ascendancy. There are unquestionably threats to identity where Muslims live as minority populations, especially in the 'sinfulness and degeneracy'

---

[28] For details see M. Cook, *Muhammad*, 20-21.
[29] K. Cragg, *The Call of the Minaret*, 176.
[30] K. Cragg, *The Call of the Minaret*, 176.

of the West.[31] There is also unquestionably something in the DNA of Islam that in such situations gives birth to what Rippin terms the 'politicisation of Muslims', and a point he makes with special reference to the 'diaspora populations in North America and Europe'.[32] France and Britain in particular come to mind as microcosms of the wider Islamic world where the urge of politicisation is enhancing unity.

Much more common in the contemporary vocabulary of the West than the term *'umma'* is the chilling term *'jihad'*. Even the most rigorously disciplined and objective non-Muslim minds cannot now dissociate the word from the almost apocalyptic images of September 11, 2001 that are seared in the collective consciousness. This event and other recent ones of comparable violence, serve as a reminder that force has been used throughout history to bring about the submission of non-Muslims and to create a unity grounded in assimilation. Although Christians have at times engaged in the most horrendous violence, including against Muslims (witness the July 1995 massacre of 8,000 Muslim men at boys at Srebrenica by Christian Serbs), there is no doctrinal justification in the New Testament for such actions, and indeed quite the opposite if the injunction of its founder to 'Put your sword back into its place' (Matthew 26:52) is to be taken seriously. But in Islam the sword has remained unsheathed, and has done so because its use finds legitimation in both the historical practice of the Prophet and in the Qur'anic texts.[33] This continuity of intent, together with its contribution to holding Islam together as a world faith, is noted succinctly by Karsh: 'Osama bin Laden and other Islamists' war is not against America per se, but is rather the most recent manifestation of the millenarian jihad for a universal Islamic empire (or umma).'[34]

In addition to what I have called inherently 'positive' aspects of Islam and others that have arguably been detrimental to the wellbeing of non-Muslims, there is a further collection of factors from beyond Islam itself that, while not creating unity, has at least

---

[31] B. Lewis, *The Crisis of Islam: Holy War and Unholy Terror* (New York: Random House, 2003), 78, paraphrasing Sayyid Qutb's reaction to the American way of life.

[32] A. Rippin, *Muslims*, 258.

[33] Mahmud Shaltut, though, is one Muslim writer who strenuously denies this association, 'The Koran and Fighting', in *Jihad in Medieval and Modern Islam*, ed. R. Peters (Leiden: E.J. Brill, 1977), 51.

[34] E. Karsh, *Islamic Imperialism: A History* (New Haven and London: Yale, 2007), 239.

bolstered it. The actual significance of these influences in terms of assigning a weighting to each is debated, but the fact that they are of *some* importance is not.

A clear memory from living in Pakistan during the first Gulf War of 1991 is of its portrayal as a new 'Crusade' against Islam. The posters in almost every shop in the bazaar reinforced this conviction – a pious Saddam Hussein kneeling in prayer, superimposed on a splendid mosque, with jet fighters flying overhead. Notwithstanding the need to view the Crusades as 'a link in the chain of history'[35], for Muslims the memory of this violence against them is ingrained in the psyche of the community. The summons to remember the Crusades is, I would suggest, of a comparable catalytic effect to the rallying cry of the Jews to 'remember Masada' following the brutalities of the Romans in AD 66. Together with Christianity's willingness to use the sword for the sake of the kingdom, there was also the completely missed opportunity to engage in mission by proclamation. With masterly understatement Riddell and Cotterell state, 'The Crusades were notable for the absence of missionary concern'.[36]

Though not viewed with the same retaliatory fervour as the Crusades, the long history of European imperialism and colonialism, and the resulting indignities for many Muslims, has not been forgotten. But without doubt, the ultimate manifestation of the anti-Islamic colonial-imperialist impulse has been the creation of the State of Israel. The loathing directed at Israel from the Islamic, and not only Arabic world, is well-captured in the term used consistently by Pakistan's daily English newspapers, the 'Zionist entity'. That there is palpable antipathy to Israel throughout the Muslim world is a truism, but the extent to which it will ultimately serve as an indirect factor holding Islam together is unknown. Rippin comments: 'Zionism has led to a strengthening of Islamic identity according to many observers, although most would also comment that even so, no united front has appeared among the Islamic nations, especially the Arabs.'[37]

My discussion has identified three distinctly different groupings of factors holding a very diverse Islam together as a world faith. While

---

[35] P. G. Riddell, and P. Cotterell, *Islam in Context: Past, Present and Future* (Grand Rapids, Michigan: Baker, 2003), 102.

[36] P. G. Riddell, and P. Cotterell, *Islam in Context: Past, Present and Future,* 101.

[37] A. Rippin, *Muslims,* 184.

each group and the specific points within each one contribute objectively to a sum total, there can be no denying the existence of a less tangible 'something else' as well, what Cragg calls 'a peculiar tenacious quality about the continuity and identity of Islam'.[38]

Bibliography

Cook, M., *Muhammad* (Oxford: University Press, 1983).

Cragg, K., *The Call of the Minaret* (Oxford: Oneworld, 2000).

Karsh, E., *Islamic Imperialism: A History* (New Haven and London: Yale, 2007).

Lester, T., 'What is the Koran?' *The Atlantic Monthly* (1999) 43-56.

Lewis, B., *The Crisis of Islam: Holy War and Unholy Terror* (New York: Random House, 2003).

Nizamoglu, C., 'Cats in Islamic Culture', 2007, no pages http://muslimheritage.com/topics/default.cfm?ArticleID=686.

Riddell, P. G. and Cotterell, P., *Islam in Context: Past, Present and Future* (Grand Rapids, Michigan: Baker, 2003).

Rippin, A., *Muslims: Their Religious Beliefs and Practices*, (3rd ed., London and New York: Routledge, 2005).

Shaltut, M., 'The Koran and Fighting', in R. Peters (ed.), *Jihad in Medieval and Modern Islam*, (Leiden: E.J. Brill, 1977).

---

[38] K. Cragg, *The Call of the Minaret*, 175.

Muslim Scholars Address the Hadith [39]

Bernie Power

The hadith are a collection of documents regarding the life and sayings of the prophet Muhammad and his companions. They were collated between 150 to 250 years after Muhammad's death based on oral reports by companions of the Prophet and linked by oral chains of transmission.

Not all hadith reports are equally accepted. Some, such as those in the collections of al-Bukhari and Muslim, are considered authentic or *saheeh*, having passed the highest and most rigorous standards of assessment. Others are considered weak or *da'eef* and therefore questioned. Still others are considered fabricated or forged i.e. *mawduu'* and therefore rejected.

You may have heard of the alleged saying of Muhammad, while returning from battle: "I am going from the lesser jihad to the greater jihad." When asked "What is the greater jihad?" He is reported to have replied: "The battle against one's soul or oneself." Melbourne social scientist Waleed Aly states: "This famous 'greater jihad' report is of highly questionable historical authenticity. It does not occur in any of the most authoritative collections of narrations of the Prophet, and probably surfaced for the first time among ascetic movements just before al-Ghazzali's time." [40] Al-Ghazzali

---

[39] This paper was delivered at a day conference held at the Australian Catholic University, Melbourne, on 4 August 2010.

[40] Waleed Aly, *People Like Us: How arrogance is dividing Islam and the West* (Sydney: Picador, 2007), 153.

died in 1111 AD, around 500 years after Muhammad lived. We are not concerned here with such spurious accounts of disputed dependability.

There are six collections generally accepted by Sunni Muslims, and my paper will draw only on the collection by al-Bukhari.

Surprisingly Muslims do not respond to these *saheeh* hadiths in the same way. Most Muslims accept them. Others will question those whose content they do not accept. Others reject all hadith. We will look at these groups in turn.

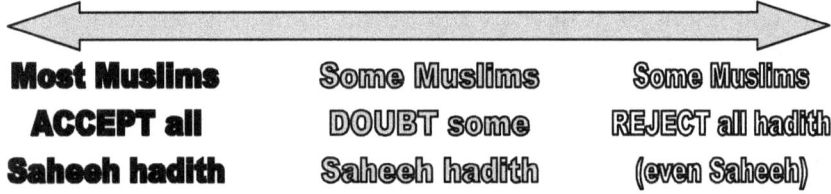

1. Most Muslims accept all Saheeh hadith

The Hadith are important for Islam since they provide a means for understanding the Qur'an. Melbourne's Abdullah Saeed notes that "[t]hese anecdotes are important in understanding what the Qur'an says on many issues. A good example of this is how to perform the five daily prayers. The Qur'an commands Muslims to perform daily prayers but does not give any details as to how, when, and in what form these prayers should be performed. The Prophet Muhammad explained the prayers in detail and showed Muslims how to perform them. These are reported in Hadith, and Muslims rely on such Hadith to understand how to perform the prayers."[41] Other key topics such as circumcision and the *shahada* are not mentioned in the Qur'an but are found only in the Hadith.

Some scholars would see them as indispensable. Fazlur Rahman says: " ... if the Hadith *as a whole* is cast away, the basis for the historicity of the Qur'an is removed at one stroke."[42] The South

---

[41] Abdullah Saeed *Muslim Australians: Their Beliefs, Practices and Institutions* (Canberra: DIMIA, 2004) 46.

[42] Fazlur Rahman, *Islam* (Chicago: University of Chicago Press, 1979, 2nd ed.), 66 (italics his).

African Council of Muslim Theologians assert that "[t]he Holy Qur'an without the Hadith or Sunna of the Prophet remains unintelligible in certain instances and in view of that, the Holy Qur'an has, in several verses, ordered Muslims to follow the Prophet in all his deeds and sayings. Therefore, if one believes in the Holy Qur'an, there is no other alternative but to uphold the Hadith of the Prophet."[43] The majority of Muslims world-wide would accept the Hadith as authoritative and normative descriptors of the life of Muhammad and therefore of their own faith.

2. Some Muslims question some Saheeh hadith

Chiragh Ali (1844-1895) may have been the earliest modern Muslim hadith-doubter, for he "anticipated Goldziher in his scepticism concerning the authenticity of even the classical collections."[44] In 1885, this Indian scholar referred to the traditions as "the inventions of a playful fantasy ...not deserving of confidence ... very few of which are genuine reports ... a chaotic sea. Truth and error, fact and fable mingled together in an indistinguishable confusion. ... I am seldom inclined to quote traditions having little or no belief in their genuineness, as generally they are unauthentic, unsupported, and one-sided."[45] His cynicism was shared by Mahmoud Abu Rayyah (1889–1970) who "adduced many arguments from different sources to undermine the position of Hadith literature. The result of his research was a book which ... tore the Hadith literature to pieces." He concluded that "the entire Tradition literature should be submitted anew to an extensive examination as to its textual reliability."[46] Equally unconvinced was Rashid Rida (1865–1935) who believed that "many hadiths of sound *isnad* should be submitted to criticism of their contents... he rejected hadiths if they appeared to him to be rationally or theologically objectionable, or if they conflicted with broad principles of the Shari'ah."

There were a range of reasons why these scholars questioned or rejected certain Saheeh Hadith. Some were scientific grounds.

---

[43] Cited in Ergun Mehmet Caner and Emir Fethi Caner *Unveiling Islam* (Grand Rapids, MI: Kregel Publications, 2002), 96.

[44] G.H.A. Juynboll *Muslim Tradition* (Cambridge: Cambridge University Press, 1983), 2.

[45] cited in Alfred Guillaume *The Traditions of Islam: An Introduction to the Study of the Hadith Literature* (Beirut: Khayats, 1966), 95-97.

[46] Mohsen Haredy "Hadith Textual Criticism: A Reconsideration" in Al-Baiyyinah Apr-Jun 2008, 34-40. http://www.witness-pioneer.org/VMagazine/v8i1/April-June2008_v8i1.pdf accessed 4th Dec, 2009.

French scientist and Muslim convert Maurice Bucaille confesses that some of the Hadith contradict scientific understandings. "The difference is in fact quite staggering between the accuracy of the data contained in the Quran, when compared with modern scientific knowledge, and the highly questionable character of the statements in the hadiths on subjects whose tenor is essentially scientific." While admitting the limited nature of early medicine, he states: "It does not seem – *a priori* – to be a very good idea, however, to suggest that people drink camel's urine." [47] This is a reference to some unusual prophetic advice: "Some people of 'Ukl or 'Uraina tribe came to Medina and its climate did not suit them. So the Prophet ordered them to go to the herd of (Milch) camels and to drink their milk and urine (as a medicine)."[48] This regimen was attested by others.[49]

Contagion through physical contact was not understood. An unconventional medical treatment is Muhammad's advice about insect contamination: "If a fly falls in the vessel of any of you, let him dip all of it (into the vessel) and then throw it away, for in one of its wings there is a disease and in the other there is healing (antidote for it) i.e. the treatment for that disease."[50] When a dead mouse was found in some ghee (butter-fat), the advice was reversed. Muhammad told the cook: "Throw away the mouse and the portion of butter-fat around it, and eat the rest."[51] Other rulings break the most basic principles of hygiene. Although a range of infections, such as gastro-enteritis, Hepatitis A, glandular fever, herpes, respiratory infections, and parasites such as giardia, can be conveyed by saliva, Muhammad is reported as telling his followers: "When you eat, do not wipe your hand till you have licked it, or had it licked by somebody else."[52] The Prophet himself engaged in the practice of *tahnik* with new-born children. "He asked for a date, chewed it, and put his saliva in the mouth of the child. So the first thing to enter its stomach was the saliva of Allah's Apostle."[53]

---

[47] Maurice Bucaille *The Bible, the Qur'an and Science* (Indianapolis: North American Trust Publication, 1979), 244-246.

[48] B.1:234; 2:577; 5:505; 7:589, 590.

[49] B.7:672.

[50] B.7:673; also 4:537.

[51] B.7:448, also 7:447, 446; 1:236, 237.

[52] B.7:366.

[53] B.7:378, also 2:578; 7:376, 377, 379.1, 450, 714; 8:31, 218.

Muslims with scientific knowledge have found these hadiths difficult to endorse.

Muslim feminist scholars have been concerned about hadiths which have an anti-women tone. These would include sayings of Muhammad such as: "I looked at Hell and saw that the majority of its inhabitants were women" (al-Bukhari .4:464; also 1:28; 2:541; 7:124, 125, 126; 8:456, 554, 555) and "After me I have not left any affliction more harmful to men than women." (al-Bukhari 7:33). It began with the first woman, for he said: "but for Eve, wives would never betray their husbands." His statements about the origin of women have been considered condescending by some scholars. One report has the prophet saying: "[A] woman is created from a rib, and the most curved portion of the rib is its upper portion, so, if you should try to straighten it, it will break, but if you leave it as it is, it will remain crooked. So treat women nicely." (al-Bukhari 4:548; 7:114). In another version of this, he added some advice to men: "So if you want to get benefit from her, do so while she still has some crookedness." (al-Bukhari 7:113) Feminist scholars such as Afro-American Amina Waduud, the Moroccan Fatima Mernissi and Pakistan's Riffat Hassan have been scandalised by such pronouncements, encouraging others to reject what they see as patriarchalist and misogynist statements.

The Pakistani scholar Ghulam Ahmed Parwez (1903-1986) formed a group called the Bazm-e-Tolu-e-Islam (or Resurgence of Islam Party) in 1938. He taught that "The life and character of the Prophet (P) represents the pinnacle of human dignity, decency, and greatness. His exemplary life is the best role model for humanity. There is no doubt about that part of the Prophet's life which is preserved in the Quran. However, in regard to the part which is outside the Quran, if there are historical narrations which contradict the Quran, or if they go against the high moral character of the Prophet (P), then these narrations are to be questioned and should not be attributed to the Prophet (P). The same applies to the lives of his companions (R)." Some actions and sayings attributed to Muhammad in the Hadith have been considered as beneath his dignity and so have been rejected. Other have questioned statements in the Hadith on the grounds of human rights and historical inaccuracies.

The Palestinian professor Suliman Bashear (1947 – 1991) wrote that "serious doubts could easily be cast not only against traditions attributed to the Prophet and Companions but a great deal of those bearing the names of successors too."⁵⁴ In 2008, Turkey's powerful Department of Religious Affairs commissioned a team of theologians at Ankara University to develop a new collection leaving out some of the hadith reports which are not in keeping with the modern world. They claimed that even some of the authorized hadiths need to be assessed and perhaps reinterpreted in order to serve the needs of modern society.

3. Some Muslims reject all Hadith, even those accepted as saheeh

The group *Ahle Qur'an* or "People of the Qur'an" was formed in Amritsar and Lahore in 1906 by Abdullah Chakralawi (d.1930). This group taught that pure Islam is to be found in the Qur'an only. One of its members, Khwaja Ahmad Din, said in 1917:"No hadith can be trusted."

One of their concerns was that the existence of the hadith casts doubt on the comprehensibility and perspicuity of the Qur'an. The Qur'an makes great claims for itself. It describes itself as 'a light (from God),⁵⁵ glorious,⁵⁶ the truth,⁵⁷ certain,⁵⁸ inspired,⁵⁹ powerful, unassailable,⁶⁰ wise,⁶¹ perfected in truth⁶² and contains no falsehood.⁶³

It also declares itself to be clear. It is a perspicuous/plain book or Qur'an,⁶⁴ for Allah made His signs clear so you can understand.⁶⁵ We (Allah) sent down/made an Arabic Qur'an so that you may understand⁶⁶ in a clear Arabic tongue.⁶⁷

---

⁵⁴ Suliman Bashear "Abraham's Sacrifice of His Son and Related Issues", 277, cited in Ibn Warraq "Aspects of the History of Koranic Criticism" in Karl-Heinz Ohlig and Gerd-R. Puin, *The Hidden Origins of Islam: New Research into Its Early History* (Amherst, NY: Prometheus Books, 2010), 238 n.58.

⁵⁵ Q.4:174; 5:15).

⁵⁶ Q.85:21.

⁵⁷ Q.32:3; 35:31; 69:51.

⁵⁸ Q.69:51.

⁵⁹ Q.10:2,109; 42:52.

⁶⁰ Q.41:41.

⁶¹ Q.10:1; 31:2; 36:2.

⁶² Q.6:115.

⁶³ Q.41:42.

⁶⁴ Q.5:15; 12:1; 15:1; 26:2; 27:1; 28:2; 43:2; 44:2.

⁶⁵ Q.2:242.

⁶⁶ Q.12:2; 43:3.

The Qur'an asserts its own comprehensibility. It is a detailed book,[68] with a detailed explanation of everything,[69] which has neglected or omitted nothing.[70]

Moreover there is a divine tafsir that is part of the Qur'an. "We (Allah) have explained everything (in detail) with full explanation".[71] "Indeed We (Allah) have fully explained to mankind in this Qur'an every kind of similitude".[72] It is explained by One who is wise & all-knowing.[73]

Furthermore it was uncomplicated. We made the Qur'an easy to understand and remember[74] and We made it easy in Muhammad's language.[75] Moreover the Prophet was enjoined to do the same. Muhammad was told to convey the message in a clear way.[76] We did not send a messenger except with the language of his people.[77]

Consequently, the Qur'an is sufficient. Muhammad can lead people out of darkness into light[78] through its clear signs or verses.[79] Allah could have supplied other books if needed (Q.18:109)

However these critics of the Hadith ask: If the Qur'an is as wonderful, clear, comprehensive, detailed, explained, uncomplicated and sufficient as it claims to be, then why should any other documents be necessary? On his death-bed, Muhammad said: 'Bring for me (writing) paper and I will write for you a statement after which you will not go astray.' Umar replied: 'The Prophet is seriously ill, and we have got Allah's Book with us and that is sufficient for us.' (al-Bukhari 1:114). This could be a kind of motto for the Qur'an-only groups.

---

[67] Q.16:103; 26:195.
[68] Q.6:114.
[69] Q.12:111.
[70] Q.6:38.
[71] Q.17:12.
[72] Q.17:89.
[73] Q.11:1.
[74] Q.54:17, 22, 32, 40.
[75] Q.19:97.
[76] Q.16:82.
[77] Q.14:4.
[78] Q.14:4.
[79] Q.22:16; 24:46; 57:9.

Ahmed Subhi Mansour (b.1938) formed a group called the Ahl al-Qur'an "to unify all those who believe that Qur'an is the ONLY source of Islam rituals, guidance and explanation of its legislations. So, it will be forbidden for anyone who adopts what-so-called Prophet Narrations (Haddith or Sunnah) to be used or adopted to express certain point of view or interpret the Holy Qur'an." Another Muslim organization, calling itself 'Free Minds' claimed that "[t]he gravest crime the self-appointed scholars who claimed to be Muslim made was to give authority to the traditions (Sunna) and the books of Sayings (Hadith) ALONGSIDE the authority of God and His messenger."

The Quranic Society of Malaysia (QSM) was established by a group of Malaysian Muslims on 11 June, 1995 at the University of Malaya, Kuala Lumpur for the purpose of calling Muslims in Malaysia and throughout the world back to the teachings of God in His final scripture, the Quran.

The highest profile assault on the Hadith came from Libya's Colonel Mu'ammar Qaddafi in July 1977. He pointed out irreconcilable contradictions within the Hadith. Of particular concern was al-Bukhari 1:30 "When two Muslims fight (meet) each other with their swords, both the murderer as well as the murdered will go to the Hell-fire." He took this to mean that Ali would go to hell for fighting against Mu'awiya. He was also concerned about the 200 year time gap between event and compilation,[80] so he pronounced the Qur'ān as the only real source of God's word.[81] When a meeting with Hizb utTahrir delegates proved ineffective,[82] a committee of scholars, led by al-Azhar's Sheikh Muhammad al-Gazoly, visited him, pointing out the dangers of such a stance. These included being branded as an infidel and renegade. Qaddafi recanted, and the Committee announced his repentance to the Muslim world.[83]

---

[80] These included Muhammad's advice to "take half of your religion from [Aisha]" contrasting with "women are deficient in mind and religion".
http://islamicsystem.blogspot.com/2009/02/understanding-hadith.html, accessed on 18th May, 2010. See also "Studies in Usul ul Fiqh" in http://www-personal.umd.umich.edu/~etarmoom, accessed on 12th Nov, 2007.

[81] Ronald Bruce St John, *Libya and the United States: Two Centuries of Strife* (Pennsylvania: University of Pennsylvania Press, 2002), 96.

[82] http://islamicsystem.blogspot.com/2007/11/refutation-of-gadaffi-others-who-reject.html accessed on 18th May, 2010.

[83] Mark A. Gabriel *Islam and Terrorism* (Lake Mary, FL: FrontLine, 2002), 60.

To conclude, Muslims have not responded to the *saheeh* hadith in the same way. Most Muslims have accepted them. However there has been a history of questioning, challenging and even rejecting the Hadith from within the Islamic umma by significant scholars for several centuries. These have come from a variety of sources, and for a range of different reasons. A challenge for contemporary Islam is how to understand the authority of the hadith in the light of these challenges.

Making of a Missionary: the Da'iyya[84]

Dr Moyra Dale

In restricted social environments, Muslim women have always used religious occasions in the home, such as Qur'anic recitations or *dhikr*[85] to gain blessing and enjoy the religiously-sanctioned opportunity to gather and talk together over a glass of tea or a meal. Now women's homes and special gatherings are increasingly being used as sites for *da'wa*, encouraging women to conform their lives and dress to prescribed Islamic norms. So a birthday party becomes a place to urge the claims of *hijab* on all the young women attending. At the same time women are moving into more public (albeit restricted) space, such as using women's areas in mosques, or giving exhortatory sermons in the women's carriage on the train system.

This paper draws on research over a period of about eighteen months in a Middle Eastern city, when I attended the women's programme in a Sunni mosque in an upper middle-class area, and interviews with the leader or *da'iyya* who had founded the programme, whom I will call Eman.

Da'wa

The word da'iyya comes from the root du'a meaning 'to call' or 'to invite'. In Islamic religious terms da'wa is "the invitation, addressed to men (sic) by God and the prophets, to believe in the true religion, Islam." It determined the Muslim community's relationship to non-Muslims: "Those to whom the da'wa had not yet penetrated had to be invited to embrace Islam before fighting could take place."[86] The contemporary piety movement relates da'wa not only to non-Muslims, but also to the duty of every practising Muslim to urge fellow Muslims to correct Islamic

---

[84] This paper was delivered at a day conference held at the Australian Catholic University, Melbourne, on 4 August 2010.

[85] Meditation on God, usually through reciting his names or songs of praise.

[86] M. Canard, 'Da'wa', in *Encyclopaedia of Islam* (Leiden: Brill, 1965, vol.II,), 168-170.

practice. Emerick puts da'wa alongside enjoining / forbidding[87] and jihad as the three fundamental duties for Muslims.[88]

Mahmood connects the recent growth of Muslim women teachers with the development of the concept of *da'wa*: "In many ways the figure of the da'iya exemplifies the ethos of the contemporary Islamic Revival, and people now often ascribe to this figure the same degree of authority previously reserved for religious scholars."[89]

Eman described the role of the *da'iyya* in even higher terms: "the *da'iyya* is the ambassador of God to people and the successor of the Messenger."[90]

Through the role of *da'iyya* women are now ascribed a role of authority and implicit leadership (*khalifat al-nabi*) that was generally reserved for men. How they take up that role is shaped by their personal context, and the competing forces of opportunity, or access to education and patronage, and opposition, whether gender-based or political.

Support
Women teachers in history

The history of Islam has included women who were leaders[91] and teachers at different times throughout its history. Aisha and Fatima are among those commonly mentioned from the time of Muhammad, but there are also examples of women teachers as well as hadith transmitters through Islamic history. Such women had to have access to education. Usually from the ulama[92] class, these women were often taught by a male relative such as their father, and sometimes also had access to private tutors. Traditionally female religious scholars were often relatives of male clerics.

---

[87] Al-Imran: 104, 110 specifically links da'wa and enjoining / forbidding: (and let there be from you people inviting to the good, enjoining what is right and forbidding what is wrong.), whereas al-Taubah:71 addresses men and women equally, 'the believing men and believing women' to be engaged in enjoining and forbidding, along with prayer and alms-giving.

[88] He lists the seven beliefs, five faith practices and three duties: *da'wa* (calling others to Islam), *jihad* (striving in God's cause) and Encouraging good while forbidding wrong (3:110). Emerick, Yahiya, *What Islam is All About* (Kuala Lumpur: A.S.Noordeen, 1997), 50, 51.

[89] Saba Mahmood, *Politics of Piety*, (Princeton: Princeton University Press, 2005), 58.

[90] Lecture handout, Thursday Lecture, 2007.

[91] Mernissi, Fatima *The Forgotten Queens of Islam*, (trans. Mary Jo Lakeland 1993, Cambridge: Polity Press, 1990).

[92] Religious scholars.

Education, a male patron, and often class, were crucial qualifications.[93]

Increased education and resources

However the recent growth in women *da'iyyas,* or missionaries, is enabled by two major factors. The first is the increase worldwide in women's literacy and education. More recently religious material has become widely available in popular media such as books, tapes and DVD's, and satellite channels. This has given women more access to information and debate around theological issues and faith duties.

Alongside these developments has been the growth in conservative Islamic movements across the Muslim world. This is both enabled by and in turn contributes to the growth of religious material in popular media. These movements prioritize religious education, including for women. Some women preachers are self-educated: but increasingly religious institutions are offering training to women. Al-Azhar University in Cairo began training women preachers in 1999.[94]

Eman's own role as *da'iyya* is enabled by support from her family. Growing up, her father combined his business trips with doing *da'wa* in local mosques. At home he called his children together for daily prayer and teaching, and encouraged them to attend the mosque programmes, including over the long summer breaks. Eman's mother also gave her daughters freedom to spend long hours at the mosque, instead of the more traditional role of staying at home and helping with domestic work. Eman's socio-economic

---

[93] Zaynab al-Ghazali (1917-2005), a famous Islamist activist in Egypt, had a father who was an Al-Azhar-educated independent religious teacher as well as cotton merchant. He encouraged al-Ghazali to become an Islamic leader citing the example of Nusaybah bint Ka'ab al-Maziniyah, a woman who fought alongside Muhammad in the Battle of Uhud. Al-Ghazali divorced her first husband because she claimed that he interfered with her 'struggle in the way of God' (*jihad fi sabil lillah*), and married her second husband with the condition that he would not stand in the way of her work of *da'wa*. Her ability to enforce such stipulations in her marriage, together with her inability to have children, freed her to take a leading role with the work of the Muslim Brotherhood in Egypt - this while teaching that Muslim women's energies should be focused on home and family. Mahmood *Politics of Piety*, (2005),180-184.
http://www.islamicthinkers.com/index/index.php?option=com_content&task=view&id=272&Itemid=26. http://www.answers.com/topic/zaynab-al-ghazali

[94] Deeb, Lara on Arab States: Rausch, Margaret on Egypt and on North Africa: Huq, Maimuna on South Asia: Ali, Souad T.on Sudan: Demirer, Yucel on Turkey: Kalinock, Sabine on Iran, Religious Practices: Preaching and Women Preachers, in Suad Joseph (ed.), *Encyclopaedia of Women and Islamic Cultures: Practices, Interpretations and Representations* (Leiden-Boston: Brill, 2007, vol.5.), 335-354. Also interview with Eman.

background and family links give her the freedom to be able to invest her time in the mosque programme. Now married to an engineer, she ably combines her role as wife and mother with a busy teaching schedule.

A Muslim woman's role as *da'iyya* is dependent on a home and social context that give her access to education: and it is also validated by prior fulfilment of her domestic responsibilities.

Opposition
Home duties and da'wa

Women find their piety defined primarily in domestic terms. So they may encounter family resistance to involvement in a programme of religious learning and teaching that takes them outside the home and domestic responsibilities. Opposition from family, especially from the husband or his female relatives, was sometimes discussed at the mosque programme. Provided women can show they are adequately carrying out home duties, they can claim moral high ground in giving attention to religious duties. Arguments from religious sources can sometimes give women more freedom to challenge traditional cultural gender restrictions.[95]

Cultural practices

The role of women in leadership is still controversial. In many Muslim women's gatherings around the world, the teaching is still given by a man. Particularly controversial is the practice of a woman leading women in prayer in a mosque when there is a man present. While this is supported by three of the four schools of Islamic law (Shafi'i, Hanafi and Hanbali), Mahmood describes the opposition faced by an Egyptian woman da'iyya who didn't interrupt her lesson to allow women to join the male imam at the call to prayer, but waited until the end, and then led the women herself in prayer.[96] Eman also follows this practice; but the imam in the mosque is supportive of her.

Kalmbach describes how a *da'iyya* in Damascus adopts conservative behavioural and teaching practices which give her the space to teach

---

[95] Afshar, Haleh, Rob Aitken & Myfanwy Franks 'Feminisms, Islamophobia and Identities,' in *Political Studies* (2003, vol 53), 262-283.
[96] Mahmood, *Politics of Piety*, 2005, 87,88.

more radical interpretations of Islam.[97] So Eman generally follows very conventional norms of deportment. Her dress outside the home or in front of non-related men[98] is always conservative, with long dark overcoat and headscarf, showing only her face. She is careful to always defer to the male leadership of the mosque and ensure that the women's voices are not heard in the male-occupied main body of the mosque. By keeping her practice conservative she avoids censure, even while disputing the teaching of the four schools of law on men as imams in mixed gatherings through a tradition[99] which defends the right of women to lead a mixed group of men and women in prayer.

Women gain the right to challenge traditional social norms of religious leadership by showing their conformity to religious social practices of dress and general behaviour, and by supporting their challenge from within the authoritative religious texts and traditions.

Political pressures

Muslim groups have an ongoing dance of engagement and restriction with the governments of the Muslim countries within which they operate. Increasingly such governments are adopting an Islamic stance, which requires validation from religious authorities within society. However in restrictive political environments, opposition has tended to find expression within mosques and conservative Islamicist groups.

For a while women *da'iyyas* attracted less attention than male religious leaders, but as their number and influence grows, they are coming under increased attention and surveillance. In Egypt women *da'iyyas* now have to have the state-issued preaching

---

[97] Kalmbach, Hilary 'Social and Religious Change in Damascus: One Case of Female Islamic Authority,' in *British Journal of Middle Eastern Studies* 35:1 (2008), 37-57.
[98] This includes anyone not in immediate family relationship (that is, father, brothers, nephews, husband, sons).
[99] This Hadith is to be found in Musnad Ahmad ibn Hanbal, Sunan Abi Dawud and other Hadith sources. It presents the following narration: (Umm Waraqah) requested permission from the blessed Messenger (peace and blessings of Allah be upon him) that if someone could perform the Adhan in her home. ... Eventually, the noble Messenger (peace and blessings of Allah be upon him) appointed an old man as a Mua'dhdhin (caller to the Prayer) for her and also granted Umm Waraqah (ra) permission to lead her household in Prayer.
http://www.mihpirzada.com/articles/canwomanbecomeimam.html, accessed 14 August 2010. Some people argue that this only gives a woman permission to lead mixed prayer in her home, but not in the mosque.

licence.[100] For a long time in Syria the secretive women's Qubaysi movement met in houses: but with their rapid growth in numbers and influence (they are said to focus on women from wealthy or influential families) the government now has opened a number of mosques to them, where their teaching can be more easily observed.

During the time I was attending the mosque, there were some months when the government ordered mosque gates to be shut for some of the time, and activities in the mosque restricted, as part of a clamp-down aimed at restricting opposition. When I recently went to visit Eman, she told me that foreign women were no longer allowed to attend the mosque programme, but only local women from near the mosque. Even the classes she had held in her home for foreign women were no longer allowed. She indicated that her home was watched and reported on, concluding that the government was nervous of international Islamic links.

Mahmood points out that the piety movement doesn't directly confront governments. However its insistence on seeking to apply Islamic norms in every area of life challenges an implicit secular position that seeks to restrict Islam to matters of religious practice and family law[101], thereby refusing a separation into matters of *'ibaada* (worship) and *'amalaat* (works).

The perceived opposition of the west to Islam also shapes *da'wa*. The call, or *da'wa*, is to the Muslim community, so that by being renewed and true to their faith they will be able to resist western incursions. And *da'wa* is also to the west, inviting them to acknowledge Islam as the truth rather than opposing it.

The Mission

The *da'wa* to women attending the mosque programme called them to:

- move beyond ritual to knowledge,
- fulfil their home responsibilities appropriately as Muslim women,
- be involved in *da'wa* themselves to their own society and beyond.

---

[100] Mahmood, *Politics of Piety* (2005), 84.
[101] Mahmood, *Politics of Piety* (2005), 46, 47.

Beyond ritual to knowledge

The emphasis on knowledge was a constant theme. Eman exhorted the women to undergird devoted practice with understanding, telling them, '*An hour's thought is better than a year's worship.*'

This teaching is not challenging the practice of the fundamental religious duties. Nor does Eman generally question the popular practice of accruing of merit or blessing through the multiple repetition of particular verses, or recitation of the whole Qur'an, in what could be seen as a semi-magical or mechanical use of text. When she teaches on "*aql* (mind) as being as or more important than *din* (religion) - Muslims throughout the community are very good at practising their religion, less good at using their mind,"[102] Eman is not placing knowledge in opposition to faith practice. Rather, in a religious framework knowledge is presented as one of the religious duties, which may have priority over other duties. "If you need learning, take the time you spend in *dhikr* to learn."[103]

Similarly, the teaching in the mosque programme does not oppose religious teachers, nor does it encourage choice outside an Islamic framework. The women should be aware of the options for choice and how to exercise them: "People were free to agree with a given judgement or not, even as they were free to take from any of the four different schools of interpretation: and they could choose different schools for different times or subjects."[104]

Din and domestic duties

Women were encouraged to attend the mosque programme. At religious feasts women would give testimonies about how the programme had helped them. Such times almost always had a discussion of family problems that made it difficult to attend, with vigorous discussion around the right of women to come to the mosque in the face of opposition from husband or mother-in-law. Eman was careful not to subvert the priority of domestic duties, which also counted as part of a woman's proper worship. "There are different kinds of worship. There is the service of the home and children, teaching the children, caring for their food and cleaning..."[105] "Education and worship in the home is more

---

[102] Eid al Adha, 2006.

[103] Thursday lecture, notes 55.

[104] Private lecture on Women and Islam, 2005.

[105] Tuesday lecture, notes 25.

important than attending the mosque;" but in the same breath she reminded the women that, "mosques and religion are for men and for women."[106] So she also insisted that the husband had no right to forbid his wife to attend the mosque, and if he did so, she wasn't wrong to resist him. "For him to order her in her prayers and her worship, he doesn't have the right in this, there are boundaries he doesn't cross." [107]

While this is accepted within Islam, it is an important shift to locate a woman's prayers and worship in the mosque. Traditionally women have always prayed at home.[108] Eman's focus is on the lectures and acquiring knowledge as a necessary part of women's worship, rather than the *dhikr* and Qur'anic recitation which also take place at the mosque.

All called to do da'wa

Eman encouraged the women to take any opportunity to be involved in *da'wa*. A series of lectures and handouts told women the appropriate behaviour and words to use at times like weddings, births, funerals. They could copy good teaching tapes and give them away, or leave pamphlets in public places for people to pick up. Those who travelled overseas for work or study, whether to the Gulf or the West, were given contacts of other graduates from the mosque, and encouraged to think about how they might contribute. Eman urged the women to respond if they saw negative comments on Islam on the internet, and to consider learning another language

---

[106] Thursday lecture, notes 13.

[107] Interview.

[108] "For the woman, it's not required of her that she pray the obligatory five prayers in the mosque. This is inconvenient for her because the woman in Islam has to dress and it's not possible in every place and time of prayer to dress completely and go out, then return and remove the clothes, and this is a problem for her, so Islam doesn't require the woman to go out to pray in the mosque." (Interview)
For men at least, congregational prayer is always preferable to individual prayer: "The Blessed Prophet said, 'Prayer in a congregation is worth more than twenty-seven prayers said alone.'" (Emerick, *What Islam is All About,* 138). However Khattab quotes the following Hadith to say: "The Islamic recommendation to offer prayers on congregation in the mosque applies to men only. The Prophet (SAAS) advised women to offer their prayers at home, in the most secluded corner of the house."
"Umm Humayd Sa'idiyyah (RA) said: 'O Prophet of Allah, I desire to offer prayers under your leadership'. The Holy Prophet (SAAS) said: 'I know that, but your offering the prayer in a corner [of your house] is better than your offering it in a closed room, and your offering it in a closed room is better than your offering it in the courtyard of your house; and your offering it in the courtyard of your house is better than your offering it in the neighbouring mosque, and your offering it in the neighbouring mosque is better than your offering it in the biggest mosque of the town'" (Imam Ahmad and al-Tarbarani; similar Hadith in Abu Da'ud). (Huda Khattab, *The Muslim Woman's Handbook* (London: Ta-Ha Publishers, 1994), 2.

so that they could engage more effectively with the west. I knew other young people learning English with missionary intent in order to relate to westerners.

However although everyone is encouraged to be involved in *da'wa*, not everyone can be a *da'iyya*. Eman offered special training for some: "We will teach girls for free, in English and computers, the outstanding girls to become well-informed *da'iyyas*, like the prophets, the best representation, circumspect, diplomatic, neat. ... No prophet has flaws. There are special characteristics for a missionary - not all people can be one."[109]

Conclusion

Contemporary *da'wa* movements offer women opportunity to move beyond domestic spheres to new physical and textual spaces. For these *da'iyyas*, the domestic is not left behind, but becomes part of an expanding sphere of involvement.

Smith discusses the shift from domestic to public sphere: "Of course, for centuries and still today, here and globally, women care for children, cook, do housework, and make other contributions to survival. It isn't that we weren't conscious or that we ceased to be subjects when we were at home doing the work of caring and cleaning. The extraordinary moment came when we saw that this was a place from which we could speak to and of the society at large, moving into a terrain of public discourse that somewhere along the line had been appropriated by and ceded to men." [110]

Eman is involved in teaching local women and sometimes expatriates, as well as lecturing in the Gulf states. She draws on the traditional texts of Qur'an and Hadith, books of *tafsir* (commentaries), alongside CD recordings and satellite programmes. And the content of her teaching moves between the everyday everynight responsibilities of women's worlds, and global discussions of the nature of Islam and the place of women within it.

---

[109] Thursday lecture: notes 54.

[110] Smith, Dorothy E., 'The Conceptual Practices of Power', in *A Feminist Sociology of Knowledge* (Boston: Northeastern University Press, 1990), 199.

References

Afshar, Haleh, Rob Aitken & Myfanwy Franks 'Feminisms, Islamophobia and Identities,' in *Political Studies* vol 53. (2003).

Canard, M. 'Da'wa', in *Encyclopaedia of Islam*, (Leiden: Brill, 1965, vol.II).

Deeb, Lara, Arab States, 'Religious Practices: Preaching and Women Preachers', in Suad Joseph (ed.), *Encyclopaedia of Women and Islamic Cultures: Practices, Interpretations and Representations* (Leiden-Boston: Brill, 2007, vol.5.) 335-336.

Demirer, Yücel, Turkey, 'Religious Practices: Preaching and Women Preachers', in Suad Joseph (ed.), *Encyclopaedia of Women and Islamic Cultures: Vol.5. Practices, Interpretations and Representations,* (Brill: Leiden-Boston, 2007), 347-9.

Emerick, Yahiya, *What Islam is All About* (Kuala Lumpur: A.S.Noordeen, 1997).

Huq, Maimuna, South Asia, 'Religious Practices: Preaching and Women Preachers', in Suad Joseph (ed.), *Encyclopaedia of Women and Islamic Cultures: Practices, Interpretations and Representations* (Brill: Leiden-Boston, 2007, vol.5), 343-346.

Kalinock, Sabine, Iran, 'Religious Practices: Preaching and Women Preachers', in Suad Joseph (ed.), *Encyclopaedia of Women and Islamic Cultures: Practices, Interpretations and Representations* (Brill: Leiden-Boston, 2007, vol.5), 339-340.

Kalmbach, Hilary, 'Social and Religious Change in Damascus: One Case of Female Islamic Authority,' in *British Journal of Middle Eastern Studies*, 35:1 (2008).

Khattab, Huda, *The Muslim Woman's Handbook,* (London: Ta-Ha Publishers, 1993, 1994).

Mahmood, Saba, *Politics of Piety,* (Princeton: Princeton University Press, 2005).

Mernissi, Fatima, *The Forgotten Queens of Islam* (trans. Mary Jo Lakeland, Cambridge: Polity Press, 1993).

Rausch, Margaret, Egypt, 'Religious Practices: Preaching and Women Preachers', in Suad Joseph (ed.), *Encyclopaedia of Women and Islamic Cultures: Practices, Interpretations and Representations* (Brill: Leiden-Boston, 2007, vol.5.), 337-339.

Souad, T. Ali, Sudan, 'Religious Practices: Preaching and Women Preachers', in Suad Joseph (ed.), *Encyclopaedia of Women and Islamic Cultures: Practices, Interpretations and Representations* (Brill: Leiden-Boston, 2007, vol.5.), 346-7.

Smith, Dorothy E. *The Conceptual Practices of Power. A Feminist Sociology of Knowledge* (Boston: Northeastern University Press, 1990).

http://www.islamicthinkers.com/index/index.php?option=com_content&task=view&id=273&Itemid=26

http://www.answers.com/topic/zaynab-al-ghazali

http://www.mihpirzada.com/articles/canwomanbecomeimam.html

Conference Report: Australia looks towards Edinburgh 2010

Peter Riddell

This year marks 100 years since the World Mission Conference at Edinburgh in 1910, and an event of celebration was held in Edinburgh in June. On October 2-3, 2009, Christian missionaries and theologians in Melbourne organised an ecumenical celebration and seminar to set the ball rolling in anticipation of the 2010 Edinburgh gathering.

A key goal of the Melbourne event was to gather a wide range of church groups to reflect the various ways that the spirit of Edinburgh 1910 has been implemented. Institutional sponsorship and support came from diverse groups: the Catholic Mission Office of the Archdiocese of Melbourne, the Divine Word Missionaries, the Columban Missionaries, the Victorian Council of Churches, the Australian Association of Mission Studies, Yarra Theological Union, the Melbourne College of Divinity and the Bible College of Victoria.

The Friday evening programme at the Salvation Army Centre in Box Hill featured rousing singing, led by a choir from the Pacific island of Tonga, where Christianity was established in the 19th century and consolidated during the 20th century by various mission groups. First came *Praise My Soul the King of Heaven*, followed by a Tongan cultural hymn and prayers. Then retired Professor Ian Breward of the United Faculty of Theology summarised some of the major issues discussed at the 1910 Conference and considered their relevance for today.

Saturday's programme was held at excellent facilities provided without charge by Yarra Theological Union in Box Hill. The morning centred around two plenary talks and two responses to each talk. The first plenary considered "Christian Mission Among Other Faiths" and was given by Canon Dr. David Claydon, past General Secretary of the Church Mission Society of Australia, who argued that "the Christian concept of salvation in God's eternal kingdom is unique; if it were not then there would be nothing worth suffering or even dying for." He stressed the importance of contextualization in mission, the need for identifying limits to that contextualization, and that dialogue "is not a means, and should not be used as a means, for Christians to announce the gospel."

Responses to Dr Claydon's paper were delivered by Rev. Merrill Kitchen, Principal of the Churches of Christ Theological College, and Dr. Stewart Sharlow of the Catholic Interfaith Committee of the Catholic Archdiocese of Melbourne. Together Dr Claydon's address and the two responses prompted a stimulating discussion, reflecting the diverse viewpoints of those in attendance.

The second lecture addressed the topic "Christian Communities In Contemporary Contexts" and was given by Dr. Ross Langmead, Professor of Missiology and Director of the School of World Mission at Whitley College in Melbourne. He pointed out that "at Edinburgh 1910 it was assumed that world mission would be from the West to the rest; if there was thought of contexts, they were regions as big as Africa or Asia." He reflected on the last hundred years of mission since Edinburgh, arguing that "a central concern of today's missiology is to allow the gospel to take shape differently in different contexts."

Reponses to his paper came from Mr Graeme Mundine, Executive Secretary of the National Aboriginal and Torres Strait Islander Ecumenical Commission of the National Council of Churches in Australia, and Rev. Jason Kioa, Uniting Church of Australia Moderator. Both developed the issue of contextualisation raised by the plenary presentations, and offered a personal testimony about the challenges the churches face in reaching out to Aboriginal and immigrant communities in Australia.

Saturday afternoon provided the opportunity to digest the discussions from the morning. Three workshops were held, two focusing on the plenary lectures and the third focusing on issues for the Church and Aboriginal people in Australia. The day concluded with a short prayer session.

Around 65 people were in attendance for the Friday evening and Saturday morning programmes, with 35 staying on for the workshops. The quality of the lectures was very high, enabling active and creative discussion to take place. The modest attendance raises issues about the level of awareness among lay Christians concerning the Edinburgh 1910 conference and the world mission that followed it. The churches face a significant challenge in raising awareness in this regard, and hopefully the Edinburgh 2010 gathering last June will have had a positive impact on stimulating interest in mission in the future.

This is an edited version of an article that first appeared in the December 2009 issue of Evangelicals Now (www.e-n.org.uk).

Christian Mission Among Other Faiths[111]

Canon Dr David Claydon

Religious narrative may inform one's identity and one's world-view, but in itself it has no impact on one's post-death situation. Whether one believes in pushing up daisies, or in eternal salvation, reincarnation or nirvana, or is committed to a view about a world of spirits, the belief will have absolutely no impact on what actually happens at the point of death! Most religious narratives offer a post-death concept and most assume some level of human achievement such as good behaviour or the killing of an infidel.[112] Yet the Christian gospel places salvation in the hands of God alone whilst inviting individuals to place themselves in a right relationship with this self-revealing God.

So those committed to the Christian narrative would have a motivation to announce the availability of salvation as grounds for announcing the Christian gospel. However, salvation is not the only ground for this announcement. St Paul made it clear as he travelled across Europe where many other religions were adhered to that there is an immediate need to see lives remoulded by the active presence of God the Holy Spirit in the life of all those who turn to God's grace.[113]

We must recognize the right of all people to pursue the world-view they choose, for there is likely to be elements of truth in their world-view, and Christians would wish that no matter what nation they live in, they too would be free to follow their religious commitment. Given that recognition, we might ask if there is anything unique in the various religious narratives. There are some areas of overlap such as between the Pharonic concept of a wealthy after-life and

---

[111] This paper was delivered at the 'Edinburgh 2010 Conference' in Melbourne 3rd October 2009.

[112] Hendrik M. Vroom, *Religions and the Truth* (Grand Rapids: William B. Eerdmans, 1989), 331. argues that the finitude is fundamental to all philosophies of life. One could also look at a Medina text such as Qur'an 9:111.

[113] For instance see Pauline letters and in particular a passage like Romans 12:1-2. Also see Vroom, *Religions and the Truth,* 329, "religious persuasion remains *alive* as long as it is sustained by experiences."

some Chinese religions[114], as well as between Hinduism and Buddhism.[115] But the Christian concept of salvation in God's eternal kingdom is unique; if it were not then there would be nothing worth suffering or even dying for. Not only our past, but also sadly our present history indicates that many people suffer and die for the sake of their commitment to the God of grace.[116] The 1910 Edinburgh conference was held to promote mission to those who did not hold a Christian Faith and we must take this into account. It assumed the potential universality of the gospel, but as Panikkar[117] has pointed out such action creates a problem for those who do not hold to this faith.

So in today's world we need to ascertain what an appropriate position could be. In arriving at this point I would first make two warnings.

There is no advantage in **patronizing others**. Each person develops a personal identity in the light of the faith adopted.[118] We as Christians do not want to show ourselves as having a superior attitude, therefore we should not patronize those of other faiths.[119] We are called by the Bible to be humble and our humility lies in the fact that human achievement is not the mechanism for attaining a changed life or eternal salvation. We are open to learning from other cultures and values[120] as well as the religious understandings of those among whom we seek to make known the Christian gospel.[121] However, we do have a unique message to present and each individual needs to make up her/his own mind from the range of messages heard as to which one will be followed.

---

[114] See for instance: David Downs, *Unwrapping the Pharaohs* (Master Books: Green Forest AR, 2006), the whole book and pp.45ff. And on Chinese religions see Ralph R. Covell, *Confucius, The Buddha, and Christ* (Orbis Books: Maryknoll, NY, 1986), 140ff.

[115] Vroom, *Religions and the Truth,* 325.

[116] See Paul Marshall, *Their Blood Cries Out* (Dallas: Word Publishing, 1997).

[117] Raimundo Panikkar, *The Intrareligious Dialogue* (Paulist Press: New York, 1978), 13.

[118] One might add also that culture has a very significant impact on identity, but the 1910 conference apparently did not reflect on culture. See S. Wesley Ariarajah, *Gospel and Culture* (WCC Publications: Geneva, 1994), 4.

[119] Superiority is a cultural product according to H. Kraemer, *The Christian Message in a Non-Christian World* (Grand Rapids: Kregel, 1956),109.

[120] The Jerusalem 1928 WCC conference placed some emphasis on values in other cultures and religions. Ariarajah, *Gospel and Culture*, 4.

[121] This point is strongly made by Kraemer, in his preface p.2 & pp 101ff.

There is no advantage in being **approvingly sympathetic** to other religious narratives. At the 1893 World Parliament of Religions in Chicago, Swami Vivekanada pursued Ram Mohan Roy's position that the Hindu practice of Sati (*Sutee*) could be dropped as this is not taught in the Vedas[122] and thus Hinduism must be acknowledged as a helpful religion.[123] If on this basis we approve the Hindu religion, then we are declaring that the Christian gospel has nothing unique to say. The same position becomes obvious when we note that regardless of what peaceful Muslims may state, their operational manual, namely the Qur'an, does declare that Islam is the only right universal religion, and apostates should be killed.[124] The old pluralistic view that there are many paths up the same mountain all leading to the top of the mountain, is not a helpful image (particularly when doctrine and political ideology merge). If there is an eternal God, then only that God can declare who he is and how he can be reached (Islam, Judaism and Christianity reject pluralism). Any human attempt at discovering the Divine has to be a product of human imagination.[125] So either we have a self-declaring God to announce or we should keep quiet. If we do make such an announcement then we do have some boundaries for we are not simply appeasers. I will comment further on boundaries in a moment.

For Christian Mission today we need to grasp some concepts.

The most widely known concept is that of **contextualization**.[126] A range of meanings have been attached to this concept. It has its roots in Paul's message at the Areopagus (Acts 17), in that he related to an existing inscription on a local altar and recognized the belief in an 'unknown God'. He was relating to an awareness of

---

[122] Swami Ranganathanda, *The Essence of Indian Culture* (The Ramakrishna Mission: Calcutta, 1965), 55-8. And David Burnett, *The Spirit of Hinduism* (Monarch Books: Oxford, 2006), 236, 249.

[123] Daniel Gold in Martin E. Marty and R. Scott Appleby, *Fundamentalisms Observed* (University of Chicago: Chicago, 1991), 535. However, this publication and the Chicago Parliament of Religions precedes the development of the Political ideology of Hindutva and its antagonism to Indians not being Hindus.

[124] Qur'an 3:85-91; 5:32; 9:5,29; 16:106 & in the Hadith by Bukhari,4:260. However some writers object to the interpretation and argue that punishment is only in the after-life – see M.M. Ali, *The Religion of Islam* (Ahmadiyya: Lahore, 1990), 438. This is an ideological stance not followed by all Muslims, but is reflected also in the Hindutva ideology.

[125] This comment is supported by Ariarajah, *Gospel and Culture*, 6, and Biblical texts such as John 14:6.

[126] A useful publication on this topic is David J. Hesselgrave & Edward Rommen, *Contextualization* (William Carey Library: Pasadena, 1989).

many of his listeners. Over the years many missionaries have found that the local people among whom they are ministering already have some awareness of concepts which need to be further developed. There are some truths in most world-views. Lesslie Newbigin embarks on this concept with a chapter in his "The Gospel in a Pluralist Society"[127]. He states that the truth about the gospel must be announced in a way that makes sense to the hearer and yet at the same time it must 'not be a product shaped by the mind of the hearer.'[128] The gospel must be conveyed in the culture in which it is being announced and not presented in its original Hebrew culture.[129] Some religions have a concept of a Creator God yet know little if anything about him. Vince Donovan discovered this in his work with the Masai.[130] Don Richardson found a redemptive analogy in his ministry among the Asmat tribe in Irian Jaya.[131] Workers among Muslims can identify with the 'One God' concept, with the belief in 'Isa' and that we represent God in the world, but in all cases there is an enormous movement away from their original understanding as the story about Jesus unfolds and the character of a loving Christ is made clear.[132] Eventually the missionary will discuss the Triune nature of God, since contextualization means both relating to already known ideas as well as sensitivity to the yet to be known. The term 'contextualization' is also used to establish a faithful declaration of God's written word and relating this meaning to the context in a meaningful way.[133]

The next concept I need to mention is the not so well known concept of **determining the boundaries**. Those in ministry today would be expected to identify the Biblical boundaries of behaviour

---

[127] Lesslie Newbigin, *The Gospel in a Pluralist Society* (William B. Eerdmans: Grand Rapids), 141-154.

[128] Newbigin, *The Gospel in a Pluralist Society*, 141.

[129] Newbigin, *The Gospel in a Pluralist Society*, 145-7.

[130] Vincent J. Donovan, *Christianity Rediscovered* (SCM Press: London, 1978), 42ff.

[131] Don Richardson, "Concept Fulfillment", in Ralph D.Winter and Steven C. Hawthorne (eds), *Perspectives on the World Christian Movement* (William Carey Library: Pasadena, 1981), 19.

[132] See Mark Durie, *Revelation – Do we worship the same God?* (City Harvest: Upper Mt Gravatt, 2006).

[133] John Travis outlined a contextualization spectrum in *Evangelical Missions Quarterly*. (4:34, 1998, 407-8) and some have opted for minimising all appearance of the Christian faith by continuing to function in one's original faith. For one argument about this see www.Lausanne.org/conversations.

linked to the nature and practice of the person of Jesus[134]. One would hope also that all those in ministry today will work within the cultural boundaries until any of these boundaries are in conflict with the nature of the person of Jesus. Those committed to some faith or to no faith usually hold to some truths and Christians need to identify these, build on them and respect the culture in which they have been formed. But Christians owe allegiance and discipline only to the Cross. This means that whilst doctrine is not changed, values may be reviewed and adjusted as needed without necessarily being in conflict with the boundaries set.

The common basis for relating to people of other faiths today appears to be on a **dialogue platform**. The assumptions about dialogue vary enormously.[135] But the essentials are firstly, that neither side expects to change its doctrinal stance. Secondly then, the purpose cannot be for conversion and it must be to convey historical facts, and/or to explain doctrinal positions[136] and/or to promote harmony among the people. In Nigeria it has been used in an attempt to persuade Muslims not to kill Christians and burn down their churches (no doubt a desire for peace) and this has been a noted failure. In Nepal and India it has been used to explain that people are not paid money to convert (an attempt to explain the facts) and this too has not been successful. In Pakistan it has been used in an attempt to eliminate the blasphemy law, but this too has failed, even at the political level.[137] In Australia it has been used to improve the understanding of two faiths which are engaging, but there has been little evidence of a helpful result either in publications or in reducing proposed acts of terrorism by extremists.[138] The desire often is to strengthen the capacity for tolerance and this could mean an improvement in relationships, but normally means a shift in values as doctrine is not adjustable. The "Common Word" was a written-dialogue by a group of Imams in

---

[134] e.g. Hebrews 12.

[135] Concepts about dialogue include 'dialogue of life', 'collaboration' as well as the traditional idea of comprehension.

[136] Panikkar argues that one can absorb some teaching from other religions and allow it to develop one's already existing beliefs. See his p.14ff. But he fails to show how this does not become pantheism, or where the boundaries are being drawn.

[137] Bishop Mano Rumal-Shah, 'Race, class, culture and Christ' in *Church Scene*, Feb 2, 1996, 11.

[138] E.g. Abdullah Saeed in *The Australian*, 7 August 2009, and *Sydney Morning Herald*, 25 August 2009, 4.

Jordan 2008 and addressed to the Pope in Rome.[139] It promoted Islamic values and required that Christians not be aggressors against Islam, with no comment about Islamic aggression past or present. Clearly, dialogue tends to be a publicity event rather than an effective means of increasing tolerance. It sometimes leads to constructive engagement, particularly in enabling the participants to better understand the stance of each faith or ideology, but it certainly is not a means, and should not be used as a means, for Christians to announce the gospel. Tolerance is an acceptable goal in dialogue, but it must not mean setting aside the doctrinal truths to which a person is committed. Tolerance should not amount to political correctness or regarding alternative religious systems as equal to one's own, but it should mean respect for those who hold other positions.

Any and every mission action among those of other faiths or of no faith should be undertaken not as a displacement concept, but as an opportunity to build on whatever knowledge and ideas the listener(s) may hold to and be open to a debate about the content of the narrative. Such debate will not change the essential features of the narrative, but may change the approach and may open up ways for further declaration of the message of a right relationship with the God who has revealed himself both in word and in The Word.

© Canon Dr David Claydon

---

[139] www.acommonword.com/

Contextual Mission: An Australian Perspective[140]

Reflections on the seventh study theme of Edinburgh 2010: 'Christian Communities in Contemporary Contexts'

Prof Ross Langmead

Of the 1215 delegates to the World Missionary Conference in Edinburgh in 1910 just eighteen were from Asia and one from Africa.[141] Most of those present saw the world through European and American glasses.

But the seeds were sown for what has become a central concern of missiology today—allowing the gospel to take shape differently in different contexts.

Contextualisation refers to the ongoing and multi-layered process of allowing the gospel to take shape in a particular context. If the Good News is to become good news for particular people it needs to speak to them within their culture, in their language and addressing their experience.

Contextual mission goes beyond what the Edinburgh conference called 'accommodation' to native customs, or 'indigenisation' through training local leaders.[142] A contextual approach expects every local church—the church in every culture and the church in every region—to examine its context and critically interact with the gospel story in a deep and ongoing way, in a journey towards expressing God's Good News in ways that reflect our cultural identity.

A Shift Since 1910

This is a huge shift from the dominant assumptions of Edinburgh 1910.

---

[140] This paper was delivered at the 'Edinburgh 2010 Conference' in Melbourne 3rd October 2009.

[141] Brian Stanley, *The World Missionary Conference, Edinburgh 1910* (Grand Rapids: Eerdmans, 2009), 12-13.

[142] World Missionary Conference, *Education in relation to the Christianization of national life: Report of Commission III*, World Missionary Conference, 1910, vol. 3 (Edinburgh: Oliphant, Anderson & Ferrier, 1910), 240-241.

First, those at Edinburgh thought in geographical terms: from the West to the rest.[143] It was 'Christendom' taking the gospel to 'the non-Christian world'.[144]

Since then, Europe has become post-Christian, and church attendance a minority activity. Since then, the centre of gravity for world Christianity has moved to Africa, Asia and Latin America. As Philip Jenkins puts it, 'if we want to visualise a 'typical' contemporary Christian, we should think of a woman living in Nigeria or in a Brazilian *favela*".[145] By the second half of the century mission was 'from everywhere to everywhere'.[146]

Second, those at Edinburgh thought in terms of continents (such as Africa), regions (such as East Asia), or countries (such as China or Japan). In the survey of world mission, published by the conference, indigenous Australians were discussed in one page and Maoris in a paragraph.[147]

Now we tend to pay attention to smaller cultural units, labelled by the Lausanne Movement as 'people groups'. There might be in the order of 15,000 of these and there might be 5,000 languages. To make things more complicated, in this post-colonial and globalised era, people move between cultures and assume hybrid identities. A student of mine introduced herself recently as Korean by birth, raised in Paraguay and now an Australian citizen.

The seventh study theme of this year's Edinburgh 2010 conference was 'Christian Communities in Contemporary Contexts'. Engaging contextually involves exploring worldview, language, customs, traditions and what gospel transformation might mean in each context.[148]

---

[143] Anne-Marie Kool, 'Changing images in the formation for mission: Commission Five in the light of current challenges—A world perspective', in David A Kerr and Kenneth R Ross (eds.), *Edinburgh 2010: Mission then and now* (Oxford: Regnum, 2009), 167.

[144] World Missionary Conference, *Carrying the gospel to all the non-Christian world: Report of Commission I*, World Missionary Conference, 1910, (Edinburgh: Oliphant, Anderson & Ferrier, 1910, vol. 1), 2.

[145] Philip Jenkins, *The Next Christendom: The coming of global Christianity* (Oxford: Oxford University Press, 2002), 2.

[146] Michael Nazir-Ali, *From Everywhere to Everywhere* (London: Collins, 1991).

[147] World Missionary Conference, *Carrying the Gospel to All the Non-Christian World*, 126–127.

[148] Edinburgh 2010 < http://www.edinburgh2010.org/en/study-themes/7-christian-communities-in-contemporary-contexts.html>. Accessed 31 July 2009.

The Australian Context

When we ask ourselves what it might mean to engage in contextual mission in the Australian context, the first thing to say is that there are many Australian contexts, just as there are many Australian cultures.

I live in Melbourne's western suburbs, where, in the simple act of taking public transport, I am acutely aware of cultural complexity and hybridity every day. There are communities of Vietnamese, of Indians and of Burmese, and older communities of Greeks and Italians. At Yarraville the young upwardly-mobile professionals and those who like to be slightly bohemian (though not too much) get on the train.

There are several aspects of Australia's national context which are important if Australian Christians are to engage with their contemporary context. We could list many, of course, but I want to at least name five areas which largely frame the Australian national context. If Edinburgh 2010 serves the global church at all, it will be through prodding churches in different contexts to explore what it might mean for the gospel to take shape in each context. It could be argued that while the Australian church has for a long time been self-supporting, self-governing and self-propagating, it is still only beginning to self-theologise. That is, a distinctly Australian theology or understanding of its mission, is yet to take mature shape, although some attempts have been made to begin the conversation.

Indigenous Reconciliation

First, a fundamental aspect of the Australian context is that we are a nation founded on an unacknowledged invasion and appalling treatment of the Indigenous peoples. I'm not sure that the average non-indigenous Australian Christian appreciates how deeply this affects who we are and whether we can feel at home in this land.

Speaking as a non-indigenous Christian, those of us who arrived after 1788 invaded this land without a treaty, shot and killed Indigenous people when they resisted, moved them off their land, introduced diseases which wiped them out by the thousands, destroyed most of their culture, treated them as invisible, discriminated against them, led many of them to despair and hopelessness, introduced many of them to alcoholism and welfare dependence, let them languish in third-world conditions, removed their children and denied their claims to land. To this day, despite the welcome apology given by the federal government in 2008 and a commitment to closing the gap between Indigenous and non-indigenous Australians, government policies ride roughshod over Indigenous voices, discrimination still occurs and they remain the most disadvantaged group in Australian society.

I agree with Norman Habel that Australia will only find its soul as a nation when the long journey of reconciliation is taken, involving personal relationships between Indigenous and non-indigenous people, symbolic actions of healing, justice, a treaty, compensation, and practical steps in health, education, housing and so on.[149] The churches have a central role in this, because reconciliation is at the heart of the kingdom of God.[150] But the challenge of this context to Australian churches is to come to terms with its mixed past in relating to Indigenous people; commit itself seriously to resourcing, training and listening to the voices of Indigenous people; and make sure that justice and reconciliation does not slip off the national agenda.

A Multicultural Vision

Second, there is nowhere more suited than Australia to aspire to a multicultural vision of the Kingdom of God, where the foreigner or stranger is welcomed (Deut 10:19) and where—as in the early church—ethnic barriers are relativised as we find unity in Christ despite our diversity (Gal 3:28).

Since 1945 nearly seven million migrants have arrived in Australia, which means that half of the population increase since 1945 (from seven to twenty-one million) has been due to migration.[151] In Melbourne 29% are overseas-born, and 25% speak a language other than English at home.[152]

With some exceptions, Anglo-Australians have tended to be over-represented in churches.[153] Fifty years ago, churches expected migrants to assimilate, reflecting national policies. Then various denominations catered for migrant ethnic congregations, meeting

---

[149] Norman C Habel, *Reconciliation: Searching for Australia's soul* (Sydney: HarperCollins, 1999).

[150] Ross Langmead, 'Transformed relationships: Reconciliation as the central model for mission', *Mission Studies* 25.1 (June 2008), 5-20.

[151] Department of Immigration and Citizenship, 'Fact Sheet 2: Key facts in immigration', Australian Government, <http://www.immi.gov.au/media/fact-sheets/02key.htm>, 2009

[152] Victoria demographics, <www.about-australia.com/facts/victoria/demographics>. Accessed 31 July 2009.

[153] Philip Hughes, 'Religion and ethnicity', *Pointers* 19.3 (September 2009), 3.

separately and often worshipping in languages other than English. The current challenge is to discern when cultural diversity is best served by meeting separately—such as when new migrants can hardly speak any English and are keen to preserve their customs and culture—and when the multicultural vision of the gospel is best served by nurturing relationships between new migrants and other groups.

Mission in a Post-Christian Society

Third, if the Christendom assumptions of Edinburgh 1910 were soon to crumble in Europe, they have also crumbled in Australia. This has always been an irreligious nation as far as non-indigenous people are concerned, with low rates of church-going despite 96% of Australians claiming to be Christian in the 1901 census. That figure has now dropped to 64%,[154] with only about 10% of Australians at church on any Sunday.[155]

In a post-Christian society the Christian church is not 'on the radar' for politicians, the media and the person on the street. Commitment as a follower of Jesus is a minority activity, seen as slightly odd. The stories of the Bible are not known or understood in literature or in daily language. The church is seen negatively, as 'yesterday's cause', tainted by scandals past-and-present and simply boring and irrelevant. As many commentators have observed, we are in some ways in a similar situation to the early church, competing in a marketplace of religious ideas. But in other ways, as Lesslie Newbigin often pointed out, mission to the post-Christian West is more challenging because of the legacy of Christendom and the failures of the church.

Newbigin's suggestion is a simple but profound one, something I've explored myself in various places. He suggests that in a post-Christian context we need to tell the story of Jesus again and to embody it in our lives.[156] Along with others I call it incarnational mission, integrating word and deed as we live into the kingdom, in the hope that in God's power the story will be heard freshly by an ignorant generation.

---

[154] Philip Hughes, 'What do the 2006 Census figures about religion mean?', *Pointers* 17.3 (September 2007), 1.

[155] Peter Kaldor et al., *Build my church: Trends and possibilities for Australian churches* (Adelaide: Open Book, 1999), 15.

[156] Lesslie Newbigin, *The gospel in a pluralist society* (Grand Rapids: Eerdmans, 1989), 182.

Engaging the Postmodern Mind

Fourth, the all-pervasive context of postmodernity provides a real challenge for Christian mission in Australia. Edinburgh 1910 occurred at the height of modernity, where faith in progress, reason, technology and universal solutions was at its peak. The twentieth century saw a seismic shift that is still difficult to pinpoint. I won't try to define postmodernity here, except to say most of us recognise it, particularly amongst younger people, but also in ourselves.

We see it in acceptance of pluralism and relativism, and in a lack of interest in grand theories or overarching frameworks. We see it in the way people choose a bit of meaning from here and bit from there. We see it in the dominance of style over substance. We see it the fragmentation of life, and the desire—even passion—to connect, whether in person or by phone, email, Facebook or Twitter. We see it in the tendency of people to judge a belief, not by whether it's true or not, but whether it works for them.

Postmodernity is clearly neither to be totally rejected nor totally embraced. We need to work harder at discerning what aspects of postmodernity resonate with the gospel—such as the desire for community— and what aspects need to be challenged, such as the suspicion of over-arching frameworks of meaning. Newbigin's suggestion of telling and living the gospel story applies here as well as in the post-Christian context. Postmodern Australians seek a personal connection and want to see faith that works, faith with its sleeves rolled up.

The Asian Horizon

Fifth, and finally, the contemporary context for the Australian church includes its unique position as a predominantly western nation on the door step to South East Asia, and beyond to Asia in general. This brings us back to the focus of Edinburgh 1910, which was global mission.

In varying ways, Australians are not Europeans. No-one is typical, but take my own case. My mother was born in Beijing and I spent my childhood years in Hong Kong. I spent my student backpacking days in South East Asia and have taken an interest in Baptist mission in India and Bangladesh. I have visited Burmese friends on the Thai-Burma border, and have taught on more than one occasion at a theological college in Myanmar. I'm an Asian-oriented Australian.

Western Christians have made mistakes in their missionary endeavours, but they should not prevent us from exploring more equal partnerships with Christians in Asia. In an increasingly global village, we are now close neighbours and South East Asia, in particular, is clearly part of the Australian context.

Conclusion

The seventh study theme for Edinburgh 2010, 'Christian communities in contemporary contexts', prods us to take Australian contexts seriously, in all their incredible variety.

Like ordinary Australians, the churches can easily forget that this nation began by dispossessing those who were here, or forget that multiculturalism asks more of the church than to enjoy a variety of cuisines. Christians can find the challenge of witness in a post-Christian society daunting, or feel disoriented by the huge shifts of the postmodern worldview. And finally the Australian church can forget to raise its eyes to the Asian horizons not far from Australia.

These are just some of the contextual factors that call us to engage patiently, energetically and in an ongoing way with the communities and cultures all around us.

Dr Ross Langmead is Dean and Professor of Missiology at Whitley College.

Communiqués

EUSEBIA Graduate Seminar in Theology in Stuttgart, Germany

Dr Markus Piennisch, Director of theological studies / Peter Wassermann, Mission Director, EUSEBIA Missionsdienste, Stuttgart

We are grateful to the LORD that we were able to conduct our first Graduate Seminar for Arab co-workers in February and March 2010 in Stuttgart, Germany. In order to facilitate communication between lecturers and students we chose English as the language of instruction during this seminar. All students and lecturers were selected and prepared accordingly. Students attending have completed their studies with a B.Th.-degree in colleges in the Middle East.

Our four students were highly motivated because they hold high positions of responsibility in their churches at home. They felt the urgent need to continue their theological and missionary education because of their need in practical ministry. Although they came from different Arab countries (Jordan, Egypt, Sudan and Algeria) they share a common background of Arab-Islamic culture. This culture is home to about 300 million Muslims. Arabic is, after all, the seventh largest language in the world and thus exercises a considerable influence among our civilizations.

Living as Christians in an Arab-Islamic environment, it is important to increase the Biblical and theological competence of the workers in the ministry through a Semitic based understanding of the Bible in order to enable them to handle the increasing pressure exerted by Islam on the Christian minority of the Middle East and North Africa objectively.

The first Graduate Seminar in Theology had its emphasis on the Old Testament. Here we find the prophetic and spiritual foundation for the proclamation of the New Testament and Christian mission – particularly for the Islamic world.

The first subject was "Biblical Theology" which brought to mind anew the fundamental interconnection within the Bible. Subsequently, "Introduction to the Old Testament" followed where the essential content of the Biblical writings was developed. For this purpose it was helpful to introduce a refresher course on "Hebrew Language" with specific comparison with the Arabic language. Then the subject "Revelation and Holy Scripture" was presented in a systematic approach to enhance the understanding of salvation as God had proclaimed it to his people. These aspects were specifically researched and developed by the students in several selected texts of the Old Testament during the course "Introduction to Bible Interpretation". At the close of our study time together, a number of Biblical-theological aspects were presented and thus the Graduate Seminar was completed.

The students were grateful for this intensive and fruitful time of learning and exchange. Our student from Algeria summarized it as follows: "... For me the most important aspect of this seminar was the fact that the courses focused upon the Old Testament. My interest was directed especially towards the importance of the Old Testament because it is the foundation with regard to history as well as to contents of the New Testament. In particular, the genealogies and lines of blessing in the Old Testament were decisive for the way in which the blessing after Abraham continued - namely through Isaaq and not through Ishmael. The courses during this seminar provided a new perception of the issues for me as well as a renewed understanding of these interrelationships."

The Islamic Republic of Britain? A Personal Odyssey

Julian Holdsworth, Director for Serving In Mission, Victoria

If the fears expressed on some Christian blog sites are to be believed, the UK is in serious trouble. And I'm not talking about the economic downturn. Some online commentators argue that within a decade or three, the UK will become virtually an Islamic republic, or at best a place where the competing ideologies of secular/liberal democracy, Islam and Christianity live in a state of constant suspicion and tribal war. While this may seem remote to our circumstances here in Australia, the questions of inclusivity, migration and democracy are very relevant and haunt us with every boatload of refugees or foiled terrorist plot.

I am an Aussie-Brit who became a citizen two years ago and have lived away from the UK as a missionary and pastor for 10 years. I returned to the place of my birth for the first time in 8 years during the New Year and discovered that the country of my birth was facing some multi-cultural challenges, particularly, on the question of Islam and democracy. While, for most people, such a question is answered by information from the media or politicians or the opinion of a next-door neighbour, my observations are more personal and local...

My first stops were with my Muslim relatives...

My older sister converted to Islam many years ago and I have various nieces and nephews who, to varying degrees identify themselves as religiously and/or culturally Islamic. Did they feel that the UK was moving positively towards Islam? The short answer is that they feel like many other minorities – intimidated at times by the dominant cultural suspicions against their faith (headwear in French schools being just one European example) and yet hopeful that the Muslim influence on the way the country is run is increasing. Indeed, if current political trends continue, one of my Muslim nephews may well become a member of Parliament at a future election and play his part in achieving these desires. His aspirations would seem to represent the moderate end of Islam and indeed his commitment to a multi-religious culture could be evidenced by his current activities: he has set up an organisation to foster inter-religious dialogue and tolerance. He has chosen to operate within the current political framework, seeing no contradiction between that and his faith. On the question of the place of Islam in the UK, one relative postured that Prince Charles (the future head of state) may have already converted to Islam, but can't admit it; others foresaw the likelihood of the sheer weight of numbers contributing to the Islamization of the UK. Some commented on the futility of violence given that the Muslim birthrate will do in a hundred years what the terrorists are striving to do anyway. Many of these comments seemed to come from a wider sense of alienation within secular culture. This sense of powerlessness seems to create a hope that if "we can just get more power, things will be better". I've observed Christians go through the same process...A few years ago, I was inundated with emails flying around Christian circles to vote for Guy Sebastian to win

Australian Idol because of "the significant influence he will have for God in popular culture". Muslims, like many Christians seem to want power and people in places of influence in order to effect change in the public sphere. They, like Christians, don't like having to wait for the mustard seeds to grow; they want to make a big impact now.

What strikes me in talking with my Muslim relatives is how rarely they interact with their Christians neighbours (and vice-versa). Like most people, they aspire for an improved world and their views of this world are full of partial truths, half-formed opinions stated as facts and some genuine human goodness. They love their families and follow their faith falteringly (as do we all). They long to see their faith more central in public life (as do we all). So I would simply make an appeal to all evangelicals: don't pigeonhole Muslims into any one media-defined category. They are not the enemy; they are people to whom we are to become neighbours – broken, flawed and not so different to us. They are people to befriend and value like any other human being, but so few of us do.

But is this all there is to say in talking with Muslims: humans, just trying to do good, motivated by a particular creed? Or are the cultural barriers and Islamic values incompatible with a liberal democracy? The answer, in this writer's view, is very often, yes, but beyond the word count of this article to justify such an argument. However, I would like to add to the debate two further conversations that shed some light on these matters: one, a cause for concern and the other a challenge...

My next two stops were with two old school friends, one of whom is a high court barrister and the other a denominational leader...

Firstly, the concerns of a lawyer.

I have a school friend who works as a barrister in the Old Bailey in London. He told me of how he was recently in conversation with a fellow barrister, a Muslim. He asked him, "When you are in the mosque, do you know who the young radicals are or those within the mosque who are likely to drift towards jihadist agendas?" "Oh yes, we know them, but we keep out of their way and don't get involved", replied the Muslim barrister. My friend then asked, "So, given your defence of the British justice system in the work you do, have you told anyone at MI5 or the police about your concerns?" The man's response was startling. "Oh no, we don't do that within our community. Effectively, it would be the betrayal of a fellow

Muslim." My friend continued: "Do you see the contradiction of working for the British justice system on the one hand and failing to support it on the other?" The man had no answer.

Therein lies the dilemma for the Muslim. Loyalty to the community of Islam seems at times to be interpreted as more important than the defence of the potential victims of terrorism. This is of great concern to those who fear for liberal democracies and ought not to be underestimated. The power of group norms to silence those who are otherwise decent people is a well known social psychological phenomenon documented since the days of the Nazis in Germany. And where group norms are reinforced throughout childhood, the effect is even stronger. However, even this common scenario can quickly become a caricature that labels all Muslim communities as potential safe havens for terrorists, if only through passivity. In recent times a Muslim father of a wannabe terrorist reported his fears over his own son's increasing radicalism. This may give hope that caricatures are often false. Indeed, I wonder if we ought not to let this example shape our views of Muslims more than the predominant media-driven fears. As Christians, we must join with those who protect many of the values of our democracy and resist all narratives that claim power and force as the means to change society. However, we must not be those who are driven by the fears that pervade our culture, particularly in its attitude to Muslims.

Finally the denominational leader.

Another old school friend who had become a leading theologian in the Presbyterian church and is a committed evangelical sat me down for coffee. I asked him about his views on immigration in the UK, particularly given the success of the right wing British Nationalist Party at the European elections. His response was wise: Did I mean Islamic migration or East European? Since I'd last seen him, more than two million east Europeans had come into the UK, far more than any other people group, albeit on European Union working visas and with no say in how the country is run. Was this a bad thing? His response (as a Scottish Presbyterian!) surprised me: "Having 2 million more Catholics in the country may well be the key to revival of the church in the UK..." And then with a wry smile, "...or at least we could pray that way."

Not a bad response for times when the environment of fear over immigration becomes shrill: pray that God would bring a great move of his Spirit amongst those who are entering the country and through them to the rest of the nation. Maybe Islam and liberal democracy are sometimes competing philosophies, but let love drive us to our knees and to our migrant neighbour's door.

Reviews

> Readers are invited to submit reviews of recent publications on the study of Islam and other faiths for possible inclusion in the *CSIOF Bulletin*.

The Story of the Qur'an: Its history and place in Muslim life

Ingrid Mattson, *The Story of the Qur'an: It's history and place in Muslim life* (Oxford: Blackwell Publishing, 2008, x + 262pp) ISBN: 9781405122580 ISBN10: 1405122587.

From the outset Ingrid Mattson makes clear her intentions as twofold: first, to produce "an academically grounded but accessible introduction to the Qur'an" (vi) and second, to provide "the perspective of a Western academic who is also trying to live as a faithful Muslim" (vi). The work is replete with copious quotes from the Qur'an, interspersed with many quotes from the Sira, the authoritative biography of Muhammad, thus reinforcing the impression of the work as manifesting both academic rigour and sympathetic engagement with Islam's most sacred text.

There is much to commend in this study. It is very well written, undoubtedly achieving the goal of accessibility to a non-specialist audience, no mean feat for any study of the sacred texts of the world's great religions. A key instrument in this success is Mattson's use of rich anecdotes, grounding the more theoretical discussion in the lived reality of the Islamic faith.

Furthermore, the breadth of subject matter covered is vast, yet it coheres throughout. Mattson initially deals with the life history of Muhammad, without whom there would be no Qur'an as we know it. Her discussion then ranges across diverse subjects: the development of written Arabic in the early centuries of Islam; the canonization of the Hadith and the formulation of Sharia Law; the emergence of Qur'anic manuscripts; the mass printing of Qur'ans;

the role of modern technologies, including the internet, in increasing distribution of the Qur'an; the early debates about the createdness of the Qur'an; the early creeds; the role of the Qur'an in protecting Muslims from sickness and evil spirits; the Qur'an in the life cycle of Muslims; and much more. The reader is thus treated to a veritable smorgasbord of topics of relevance to Qur'anic Studies.

Of particular interest is that Mattson provides the perspective of a Western woman on the Qur'an and the faith that springs from it. She is a former Catholic convert to Islam, so she brings to the study a Western educational and cultural background rooted in gender sensitivity, which is supplemented by a deep study of her adopted faith. This results in some invaluable observations, such as the statement that the Isra'iliyyat, Judeo-Christian traditions which have crept into Islam down the centuries, are sometimes undermining of Qur'anic values, especially "those related to women." (194). There is much literature on the Isra'iliyyat, but this observation opens a new window into the subject which calls for further research.

Notwithstanding the strengths of this volume, weaknesses must be noted. Mattson's passing engagement with approaches to the Qur'anic text of a more critical, revisionist nature is at best half-hearted. She could have been more daring in asking some of the taboo questions if she was really seeking to persuade a Western academic audience. What about the view of many that the Qur'an is not "revelation", but is rather an evolved text which underwent the same kinds of textual "corrections" as did other great works of literature? What about the perspectives of those for whom Muhammad was not a prophet of God but was rather a skilled orator, an accomplished community leader and a fearless warrior? To address these questions, a more intentional engagement with non-Muslim revisionist scholarship would have helped, rather than her relatively brief references to such sources, largely dominated by an apologetic tone, at different points of the volume.

The first two chapters seem to be designed to smooth out the bumps of Islamic scripture and theology, explaining away those uncomfortable elements which run counter to Islamic dogma. An example is Mattson's treatment of the Satanic verses reports (52), which she presents as lacking in validity. The approach of apologetics is also seen in the discussion of the emergence of the jihad doctrine, which is portrayed as entirely reasonable. In this context, Mattson explains away the early Muslim treatment of

Jewish tribes, carefully avoiding the debate surrounding purported anti-Semitic ingredients in the early Muslim texts

To be fair, Mattson's study does become more believable as she moves down the centuries. Chapters Three to Six are more deserving of a place on undergraduate reading lists than the first two chapters. However, the quality does dip again in the Conclusion, which, like the early chapters, is more devotional than scholarly, serving a purpose of Islamic mission as well as reflecting scholarly endeavour.

There was a time when most books on Islam and its sacred text that were studied in western universities were written by non-Muslim scholars. Those days have gone, and deservedly so. It is important that western university students listen to Muslim voices and perspectives as they study Islam. Mattson's volume is a valuable resource in this regard. But this work also reminds us just how important it is that such students can continue to make reference to non-Muslim writings on Islam as well, so that the sympathetic approaches of Muslim scholars will be supplemented by other approaches, at times more critical, to ensure the continuation of western scholarly traditions where any questions can be asked, and any criticism aired.

Peter Riddell

The Banquet: A Reading of the Fifth Sura of the Qur'an

Michel Cuypers, *The Banquet: A Reading of the Fifth Sura of the Qur'an* (Convivium Press, Miami, Florida, 2009, 565 pp) ISBN 978-1-934996-05-8.

The Banquet is not just 'a' reading of Surat al-Ma'ida, but a highly significant demonstration of how to interpret the Qur'an according to its own genre. For many it may seem that the work has broken on to the scene of Qur'anic scholarship out of a vacuum. In fact the author has been meticulously applying the tools of rhetorical analysis, as defined by the Biblical scholar Roland Meynet, for some fifteen years. Most of his earlier work has, however, been published in journal articles, in French, and has dealt with shorter suras in the latter half of the Qur'an.

The book explicates a methodology that respects the way in which meaning is bound up with structure in Semitic discourse. Cuypers sets out identifiable rules at the beginning, and then, through tracing the ways in which the text adheres to them, shows how they lead to interpretative insights. Because of the way chiasms and formulaic crescendos imply distinction between universal principles and contingent particulars some of these insights challenge traditional understanding. The careful close work, paying attention to word clusters, has also resulted in identifying well substantiated intertextual resonance between Qur'anic passages and portions of both the Hebrew Bible and the New Testament. Cuypers is sensitive to the way the biblical texts work in their own contexts, and so able to draw attention to the co-incidence of interests of the Deuteronomic material which anticipates entry into the Promised Land, and the Johannine Farewell Discourse material which looks to the establishing of a new faith community. Thus, in an almost understated way, the author proves a discerning guide to underlying interests of the sura.

The copy editors failed to pick up a number of places where a computer auto-correct has opted for 'sure' instead of sura, and a half bracketed statement is left incomplete on p280. Other than these small matters the book is beautifully set out, with layout bespeaking the attention to detail to be found in the content. It is receiving warm interest in the world of Qur'anic studies, with Shi'ite and Sunni scholars affirming that the approach is in accord with the principles of qur'anic *nazm* (form). Having already become recommended reading for students engaged in Qur'anic studies at SOAS, London, *The Banquet* seems set to become a valuable entrée for those looking for ways to approach the Qur'an with integrity.

Carol M. Walker
London School of Theology, Centre for Islamic Studies

Approaches to the Qur'an in Contemporary Indonesia

Abdullah Saeed (ed.), *Approaches to the Qur'an in Contemporary Indonesia* (Oxford University Press: USA, 2005, 252pp) ISBN-10: 019720001X.

Indonesia has long been recognised as the most populous Muslim-majority nation in the world. Nevertheless, it has not traditionally exerted a level of influence on developments in world Islam commensurate with its size. This is largely because the vast majority of the scholarly output in the study of Islam emerging from Indonesia is written in the national language, Bahasa Indonesia, which does not have a significant readership beyond Southeast Asia.

In this context, this volume drawn together by Professor Abdullah Saeed serves as a valuable bridge between internal Indonesian discussion about the Qur'an and such discussion taking place in the rest of the Islamic world.

Professor Saeed has assembled a set of Indonesian Islamic writers who represent both established voices and emerging young scholars. The former include famous names such as the late Nurcholish Madjid and Azyumardi Azra while the latter include promising new voices such as Ratno Lukito and Ro'fah Mudzakir, among others. To this list of Indonesian contributors is added two distinguished names from outside the country: Professor Saeed himself, who contributes a valuable introduction, and Professor Anthony Johns, who provides an excellent chapter surveying the history of and approaches to Qur'an commentary writing throughout the Indonesian-Malay region.

The chapters themselves fall into three general groups. Professor Johns' chapter leads into a series of contributions which deal with matters generic to *tafsir* and consider three prominent Indonesian scholars: Hamka (d. 1981), Quraish Shihab (b. 1944) and H. B. Jassin (d. 2000), who produced a controversial translation of the Qur'an into Indonesian.

Chapters 7-9 then consider various themes emerging from the Qur'an: sacred versus customary law, and women's issues (polygamy and abortion).

The final two chapters then address matters of some controversy: the use of the Qur'an to advance political causes, both legitimate and non-legitimate, and the Qur'an and religious pluralism.

The book provides an important window into the kinds of concerns preoccupying Indonesian Islamic scholars today. Of particular significance is the effort to draw on the Qur'an as a source of wisdom and guidance for resolving the challenges of the modern world. Such is a matter of great discussion among Indonesian scholars of diverse persuasions, and this is ably captured in this book. The Islamic universities (formerly IAIN) are key arenas for this quest to relate the Qur'an to today's world, and this explains the preponderance of contributors who come from this Islamic university sector.

In his introduction, Professor Saeed defines the goal and anticipated audience of this work as being to "make available to an English-speaking audience a sample of writings on Qur'an-related topics by intellectuals from the world's most populous Muslim country ... and by a range of Indonesian authors" (p. 1). It is important to reflect on the success of this stated goal. This book does indeed make available in English scholarship from established and emerging Indonesian scholars. But it does so somewhat selectively, and herein lies the weakness in what is otherwise an excellent volume.

While this work provides a very solid platform for more liberal Islamic thinkers to air their thoughts – many of whom are active in various ways in Indonesia's Liberal Islam Network – these are not, of course the only kinds of Muslims who are trying to relate the Qur'an to their daily needs and challenges in Indonesia today. Indeed, there has been a notable resurgence of radical Islamist thinking in Indonesia over the last two decades, most infamously represented by militant groups such as Laskar Jihad, Front Pembela Islam, as well as by several small political parties, in addition to militant journals such as *Sabili*. Their approach to the Qur'anic text tends to be literalist, selecting verses which reinforce their own particular agenda. Yet these voices are not heard directly in this volume (though the paper by Azra does provide a window, albeit negative, into such approaches). As unwelcome as their views might be, they should nevertheless have been heard in a volume which purports to show how Indonesian Islamic thinkers approach the Qur'an and apply it to the needs of today. More of a debate within the pages of this volume between progressive liberals and more militant voices would have enhanced it considerably.

Notwithstanding that criticism – one which also applies to many recent volumes on Islam intended for a western audience – this work still makes an important contribution to Western understanding of Islam, especially within an Indonesian context.

Peter Riddell

Innovation, Tradition, and Justice: Islamic Legal Thought in Modern Indonesia

R. Michael Feener, *Innovation, Tradition and Justice: Islamic Legal Thought in Modern Indonesia* (Cambridge University Press: New York, 2007). ISBN-13: 9780521877756.

Michael Feener had already published an impressive number of articles in reputable journals and books, prior to this published version of his PhD. In his previous shorter length publications, Feener maintained a very high standard of scholarship throughout. This volume maintains that excellent standard of scholarship.

Feener has selected a substantial number of individual Indonesian Islamic writers from the 20th century to provide the backbone of his study into Islamic legal thought in Indonesia. Some of those writers have received extensive previous scholarly attention: Hasbi Ash Shiddieqy, Mohamad Natsir, Nurcholish Madjid. Others have been less studied: Moenawar Chalil, Anwar Harjono, emerging writers from the modern day. In engaging with the more famous writers, Feener succeeds in opening new windows into their literary output; hence his extended discussion of Mohamad Natsir has a freshness which is unexpected and most welcome. As for his treatment of emerging writers, he has identified significant names of the future and his presentation of their writings is a valuable contribution to the study of contemporary Indonesian Islam.

The decision to focus on Islamic legal thought as the unifying theme works. It provides the road map throughout the volume. It also ensures that Feener engages with some of the most acute and hard fought debates of 20th century Indonesian Islam, such as the fraught issue of whether or not Indonesia was to be an Islamic state after independence in 1945. Nor is that theme a mere detail of history. The debates emerging from Islamic legal thinking continue to preoccupy Indonesian Islamic scholars today, as is amply demonstrated by Feener. So the volume has clear relevance for Indonesia's past, present, and future.

The volume is well written and is easy to read. It provides much information of interest to the specialist in Indonesian Islam, while still being accessible to the intelligent non-specialist. It contains substantial originality – easily justifying the earlier award of the PhD – while at the same time cohering with, and complementing, other recent related studies (Azra, Laffan, Mobini-Kesheh). The extensive source base drawn on by Feener, reflected in his bibliography, means that this study will serve as a significant window into the field for future researchers. In short, this is a landmark study.

Peter Riddell

God's Battalions
Rodney Stark, *God's Battalions* (HarperOne Publishers: New York, 2009). ISBN 978-0-06-1582. (Available in Australia at Koorong Books).

Very few people have much good to say about the Crusades nowadays. Most think it was a terrible blight on Christian history, and cannot be condoned or justified in any way. Certainly during the past few centuries, Christianity has been attacked, and people have sought to discredit the faith, partly on the basis of the Crusades.

In such an atmosphere, this new book by Rodney Stark is as about as revolutionary as they come. He takes head on myth after myth surrounding the Crusades, and makes the case that the Crusades not only had their place, but were in fact in many ways justifiable. He clearly demonstrates that modern histories about the Crusades are among the great hatchet jobs of recent times.

Dispelling the many myths about the Crusades takes guts, and someone with the right intellectual and academic qualifications. Stark is certainly the man for the job: he has become one of our finest writers on the sociology and history of religion, and is unafraid to go against the tide.

In this important volume he debunks the historical revisionism (which is often coupled with anti-Christian bigotry) about the Crusades to offer us a more sober and clear picture of what in fact took place. He notes that it was especially during the time of the Enlightenment and onwards that critics claimed that the Crusaders were mainly Western imperialists, those who set out after land and loot.

Moreover, the contrast is often made between the bloodthirsty barbaric Christians, and the peace-loving Muslims. But as Stark persuasively documents, none of this is close to the truth. The real story is this: the Crusades were certainly provoked, and the Crusaders were mainly concerned to free the Holy Lands from Muslim oppression and to protect religious pilgrims who travelled there.

Indeed, to properly understand the Crusades, a lot of background information needs to be considered. That is why Stark spends the first hundred pages of his book looking at the 600-year period of Muslim conquests and dhimmitude.

The story of course begins in the seventh century when Muslim armies swept over the Middle East, North Africa, and southern Europe. One Christian land after another was attacked and conquered by advancing Muslim forces.

Stark reminds us that Muhammad told his followers, "I was ordered to fight all men until they say 'There is no god but Allah.'" Therefore a century after his death vast swathes of territory hung under the bloody sword of Islam.

And what of the conquered Christians living under Islamic rule? They, along with Jews, were known as dhimmis. While revisionist historians and Muslim apologists speak of Muslim tolerance here, the "truth about life under Muslim rule is quite different".

Indeed, the subject peoples had few options: death, enslavement or conversion were the only avenues open to them. Dhimmitude was no picnic. Death was the fate of anyone who dared to convert out of Islam. No churches or synagogues could be built. There was to be no public praying or reading of Scripture. They were at best treated as second-class citizens, and at worst, punished and killed.

And massacres of Jews and Christians were quite common in the centuries leading up to the Crusades. In 1032-1033 in Morocco alone, there were over six thousand Jews murdered. Jerusalem fell to the Muslims in 638. The Dome of the Rock was built from 685 to 691, and churches and synagogues were levelled in the ensuing centuries.

The condition of Christians in Jerusalem was pretty appalling during this period, as was the plight of penitent pilgrims seeking to enter Jerusalem. They suffered much persecution, and risked their lives simply to travel to the holy city. The destruction of the Church of the Holy Sepulchre – along with thousands of other Christian churches – under the bloody reign of the Fatimid Caliph Abu Ali al-Mansur al-Hakim at the end of the first millennia simply served as the climax to all this misery and outrage.

It is in this light of six centuries of Islamic conquest, bloodshed and tyranny that the Crusades must be viewed. They were not always pretty, but life in general back then was not pretty. If Crusader excesses took place, this was just par for the course, as excesses by Muslims and others were more than commonplace.

As Stark reminds us, "Granted, it was a cruel and bloody age, but nothing is to be gained either in terms of moral insights or historical comprehension by anachronistically imposing the Geneva Convention on these times."

He looks at the various Crusades, dealing with the host of mythologies that have grown up around them. One is the fanciful depiction of Saladin as some gallant, humane Muslim resisting those bloodthirsty Christians. For example, when he re-conquered Jerusalem in 1187, the city was spared a massacre.

But the rules of warfare back then stipulated that cities would be spared if they were not forced to be taken by storm. So while bloodshed was limited, "half the city's Latin Christian residents were marched away to the slave markets".

And as Stark reminds us, Jerusalem was the exception to Saladin's normal style. Savage butchery of his enemies was his usual habit. Indeed, he had been looking forward to massacring the inhabitants of Jerusalem, but a compromise was struck which prevented this. But he had plenty of other opportunities to let the blood flow freely, often at his own hand.

Then there is the myth that the Crusades have been a longstanding grievance amongst Muslims. Not so argues Stark: "Muslim antagonism about the Crusades did not appear until about 1900, in reaction against the decline of the Ottoman Empire".

Christians today can well argue whether the Crusades were in fact warranted. But any such discussion about the pros and cons of the matter must be made under a clear understanding of what exactly transpired and why. This book admirably serves that purpose, and must be the starting point for any future debates over the topic.

Bill Muehlenberg
CultureWatch (http://www.billmuehlenberg.com/)

World of the Spirits

David Burnett, *World of the Spirits: A Christian Perspective on Traditional and Folk Religions* (Oxford: Monarch Books 2000, reprinted 2005, 287pp) ISBN 9-781854-247421.

This work first appeared in 2000, but its reprinting in 2005 shows that the approach taken by the author still has considerable currency. It represents a substantial revision with a new title of the author's *Unearthly Powers* (MARC, 1988), taking account of Burnett's own further thinking as well as increasing attention to traditional religions by the scholarly community.

Content

The opening chapter includes a useful survey of developments in anthropological thinking and methodology, moving from earlier paternalistic approaches by Western analysts of "primitive" societies to more recent approaches that respect the societies and faiths being studied, allowing them to speak for themselves rather than being expressed through the prism of western and Christian frameworks. Burnett emphasises the importance of terminology, preferring the term "traditional" religions rather than "primitive" religions or "animism".

The second chapter undertakes a searching critique of Western, and Christian, scholarly writing on traditional religion perspectives of supreme deities and lesser spirits. The author suggests that Westerners are frequently prisoners of their own worldviews: "it is not surprising that Western scholars have too often formed ... oral accounts into a pattern that reflects a Western analysis rather than the dynamic accounts of the people themselves" (29).

Chapter 3 examines three traditional societies and their views of human nature. These societies place an emphasis on community; the view of the soul is complex; they embrace the "soul-stuff" idea where certain physical aspects are connected with deeper spiritual functions. The author contrasts these views with the Western understanding of human nature where "a clear duality has ... emerged between the material body and the mind." (47)

This is followed by a broad sweep of traditional societies, surveying the widespread belief in ghosts and ancestral spirits. The author also examines biblical teaching, pointing to evidence of belief in such a supernatural realm by certain biblical personages, e.g. Job. Also considered are "forbidden things" in traditional religions: taboo, pollution and sins, offering some cross reference to the Bible.

Chapter 6 surveys developments in anthropological thinking with regard to three kinds of ritual in traditional religions: lifecycle rituals (birth, puberty, marriage, death); calendar rituals (harvest, Christmas, Easter etc.); and rites of crises (sickness, disease, war, disasters etc.). The author considers debates among Christians regarding whether Christian converts should participate in the rituals of their original faiths.

Chapters 7 to 11 address various aspects of the spiritual realm in traditional religions. Burnett asks a key question: how do adherents of different religions deal with multiple options? While secular societies have developed various management techniques, traditional societies uses divination of different forms: mechanical methods, such as cowrie shells, throwing strips of leather onto a skin and so forth; augury, such as reading animal entrails and throwing lots; and spirit mediumship, such as the ancient Greek Delphi oracle. The author points out the rising popularity of divination in the modern world through astrology.

Chapters 8 and 9 consider witchcraft, sorcery and magic, all highly complex phenomena. Traditional societies consider these phenomena as means to identify the causes behind misfortunes: why did the crops fail, why did a child die? Also considered is the issue of witchcraft through Christian history, as seen in the witch-hunts of medieval times. Various missionary responses are presented, from a more secularist denial to Pentecostal demonic delivery approaches. In a helpful discussion of sorcery, Burnett identifies three aspects to this phenomenon: the evil eye, a widespread phenomenon throughout the Muslim world; curses; and magic rites.

While anthropologists typically take a relativist position towards spirit possession, medical practitioners and missionaries are often called upon to address it as a problem. Burnett points out a key distinction between spirit possession as an affliction and spirit possession where the afflicted gains control over the spirit and uses it to heal, thereby becoming a shaman. An extended discussion of the latter phenomenon is presented in chapter 11.

After painting a portrait of the broad features of traditional religions across diverse societies, Burnett changes the mood in chapter 12 by addressing the fraught topic of the impact of European expansion upon traditional societies. In this chapter he considers conquest, the effect of European diseases, European slave trade, and colonisation.

The final four chapters turn their attention to different results of the interaction between European and traditional societies. The first is religious conversion, initially considered by colonial era scholars as a change from primitive towards "higher" world religions, but from the 1940s treated with more sensitivity and respect for the traditional religions being discussed. Chapter 14 addresses Allison's contrast between High and Low Religion, with fascinating Hindu, Islamic, and Buddhist case studies from village India, village Java, and Sri Lanka respectively.

Chapters 15 and 16 focus on various new religious movements arising from the intermixture of European and traditional faiths, from phenomena as diverse as Haitian Voodoo, various millenarian movements and cargo cults of the Pacific, to a number of new expressions of Christianity, including the African independent churches and various movements within mission Christianity.

Assessment

There are a number of weaknesses in this work that could be addressed in a further edition. The first relates to a certain stereotyping of "the West". It is surprising that an author so concerned to emphasise diversity in the Other – traditional societies in this case – can so evidently stereotype of "the West". Many examples exist; one will suffice: "… even Western society with its strong adherence to materialism still retains some belief in ghosts." (59) Such a statement ignores the dynamic variation within Western societies such as the author presents so effectively for traditional societies. Of course, such negative stereotyping of the West is extremely common in modern scholarship, resulting in no small part from the wave of anti-westernism that developed from influential writings such as Edward Said's "Orientalism".

Another common stereotype that has assumed "sacred cow" status in scholarly discourse relates to portrayals of European colonialism. This can be seen in Chapter 12, the weakest chapter in an otherwise commendable volume. The broad-brush approach adopted by the author neglects the great variety of European colonial policies; for example, the policies of the British in Malaya were hugely different from those of the Spanish in Latin America. Burnett sees European colonialism as unique: "Although through history larger nations have impacted and conquered smaller communities, what happened with the European expansion was essentially new in its extent and impact"(196). Such a statement is a furphy, of course, and understates the extent and impact of previous great empires, such as those of ancient Greece, Rome, China and Persia. Furthermore, no mention is made of Muslim imperial expansion in the 7th-9th centuries, which was arguably the most successful case in history of empire, where the vast majority of the conquered came to identify themselves, ethnically, linguistically and religiously with their Arab conquerors. Today the Arab world stretches from Morocco to Yemen; in the 7th century the term only applied to part of the Arabian peninsula.

Another area that could be addressed in a further edition is the Insider/C5 Movement approach to extreme contextualisation. Burnett does engage with contextualisation at various points of this study, as well as with the concept of religious syncretism, so consideration of the Insider Movement would be appropriate. A hot topic one decade after this book was written, it was already very present as a debate in 2000 so its omission is surprising.

Finally, the book suffers from several unfortunate typographical errors at key points. For example, Maori is misspelt as Moari (36) at an important point of discussion of this particular community. Furthermore, the Muslim clerical figure of *imam* is misspelt as *iman* (237).

Notwithstanding the above criticisms, any assessment of this book should first and foremost measure the content against the author's three stated aims (25-26): first, to build respect for the societies and faiths beings studied; second, to help Christians understand the faiths and societies being studied in terms of their own belief system; and third, to show the patterns of transformation experienced by traditional societies in recent centuries.

Burnett achieves each of these aims admirably. But the work has other qualities as well. It serves as a very helpful introduction to the field of anthropology, especially for mission studies students. It succeeds in using a chatty style while also being sufficiently scholarly to gain the confidence of the reader. The author is energetic in engaging with a wide range of previous scholarship, as well as a wide array of religious traditions. As such, this work is a rich resource in itself, demonstrating the impressive breadth of knowledge by author. It would be well suited as a textbook at early undergraduate level for students in theological colleges and seminaries.

Peter Riddell

The Wedding Song

The Wedding Song (Le Chant des Mariées)[157]. Released 2009, Director: **Karin Albou**, Writer: Karin Albou, Country: France / Tunisia Language: In French and Arabic with subtitles, Runtime: 100mins, Broadcast on SBS 11 November 2009.

This excellent film, set in Tunisia in 1942 during the German occupation, focuses on two 16 year old girls, Myriam (Jewish) and Nour (Muslim). Both their families are poor; Nour because that is her family's lot, and Myriam because she and her mother have fallen on hard times after the death of her father. The two families live in adjoining apartments overlooking the same courtyard in the alleyways of Tunis, where the two girls have grown up together, developing a strong sisterly bond and sharing secrets and dreams of love. Myriam has been to school and is literate; Nour has not attended school, so Myriam has taught her to read Arabic. The girls consider their different religious faiths as being of no consequence to their friendship.

Each girl is to be married off by their families: Myriam to Raoul, a prosperous Jewish doctor, and Nour to Khaled, an unemployed cousin. Myriam resists the match with Raoul; Nour wants to marry Khaled but her father will not permit the marriage until Khaled finds work.

With the arrival of the German occupation forces, problems develop. Anti-Semitic German propaganda fills the radio, calling on Muslims to shun their Jewish neighbours and colleagues. The Germans levy a huge tax on Jews, triggering Myriam's mother to press her teenage daughter to marry Raoul quickly, as he has undertaken to pay their tax.

Meanwhile Nour has midnight trysts with Khaled on a rooftop, while Myriam covers for her. In order to gain Nour's father's acceptance, Khaled finds work as an informer with the Germans, helping to identify Jewish families. Myriam's house is ransacked

---

[157] Trailer: http://www.youtube.com/watch?v=enrLKs8IVuo

and her mother assaulted by German troops guided there by Khaled.

Myriam tells Nour of Khaled's role with the Germans; Nour's scepticism causes a decline in their friendship. Khaled increasingly echoes German anti-Semitic propaganda and insists that Nour stop seeing Myriam. Seeking guidance, Nour consults her father's copy of the Qur'an and comes across two key verses, Sura 2:6-7:

> As to those who reject Faith, it is the same to them whether thou warn them or do not warn them; they will not believe. Allah hath set a seal on their hearts and on their hearing, and on their eyes is a veil; great is the penalty they (incur).

This is a key moment in the film; the Qur'an, as the Word of Allah, seems to Nour to be condemning Jews, including her friend Myriam. Nour increasingly adopts the anti-Semitic discourse of Khaled, and confronts Myriam about the perceived advantages of the Jewish community:

"Why can you go to school, and I can't go?" demands Nour. "Why do I wear the veil and you don't? Why can you go outside the house without anybody commenting? You're different Myriam."

Myriam meets her mother's wishes and marries Raoul, but their wedding night is a disaster. Raoul shows compassion and accepts the need to proceed slowly.

Meanwhile Nour's father sees Nour reading Qur'an 2:6-7. He points Nour to another verse which is more affirming of non-Muslims: Q2:62

> Those who believe (in the Qur'an), and those who follow the Jewish (scriptures), and the Christians and the Sabians,- any who believe in Allah and the Last Day, and work righteousness, shall have their reward with their Lord; on them shall be no fear, nor shall they grieve.

Nour is reassured that Allah does not condemn Jews after all, and seeks reconciliation with Myriam. The film ends with Nour's wedding with Khaled. She uses the moment of their intimacy to tell him that Allah does not hate Jews and that she is maintaining her friendship with Myriam. In response, Khaled states firmly that it is he who will decide, and that she will not remain friends with Myriam. The film thus concludes on a contrasting note: Khaled's chauvinistic recalcitrance suggests problems in the future for his marriage whereas Raoul's compassion suggests that he and Myriam will overcome their problems.

The overriding patriarchal context of Tunisia in the 1940s is a dominant theme of this film. This is emphasised in interview by the talented Karin Albou, writer, director and actress (Tita) in this film: "[The girls] are two different identities, one Jew and one Muslim, but they are culturally the same – Tunisian. They have a lot in common, especially in terms of their situation as females. That's what I wanted to show ... the patriarchal domination imposed on these girls is the same for the Jewish girl as it is for the Muslim. Some people have a kind of nostalgia for that patriarchal period. I think it is important to show what is was really like."[158]

Another important theme emerging from this film is the different situations for Jews and Muslims in 1940s Tunisia. The French and the Jews had been the intellectual and economic elite of the country prior to the war. The Jews had greater freedoms than Muslims, largely because the status of Tunisia as a French protectorate meant that the Tunisian Jews benefited from the movement for emancipation among the Jews of France. Jewish girls could more easily go to school than the Muslims girls, who were kept at home by their male-dominated families.[159]

However, a further key theme is largely ignored by reviewers. It relates to the role of Nour's Islamic faith and its holy book, the Qur'an, which is shown to be clearly ambiguous about Jews (and other non-Muslims). So one verse leads Nour to adopt Khaled's anti-Semitic views (which themselves echo the non-Scripture driven prejudices of the German occupiers), while another Qur'anic verse leads Nour in the opposite direction of reconciliation with Myriam, her Jewish friend. Thus while one source of anti-Jewish prejudice, the German occupiers, is there for a time but then disappears forever, the ambiguous role of the Qur'an as a source of anti-Jewish sentiment remains, leading some (Nour and her father) to embrace their Jewish neighbours as friends but potentially leading others to adopt the prejudicial views of Khaled, who refuses to recant.

This is an excellent film from the perspective of entertainment. But it is much more than that.

---

[158] http://www.youtube.com/watch?v=ujT_dYOULqI&NR=1&feature=fvwp

[159] http://www.youtube.com/watch?v=ujT_dYOULqI&NR=1&feature=fvwp

It provides a window into past history through its snapshot of Tunisia in 1942. But it also provides a window into the future, by laying before the reader those Qur'anic ambiguities that lead some more literalist Muslims to embrace extreme prejudices against Jews and other non-Muslims, a topic of great relevance to today.

Peter Riddell

The Third Choice

Mark Durie, *The Third Choice* (Deror Books: USA, 2009) ISBN: 978-0-9807223-0-7 Paperback, ISBN: 978-0-9807223-1-4 Hardback.

Anything Mark Durie writes is well worth reading. His latest book The *Third Choice* is no exception. Here he breaks new ground in uncovering from texts ancient and modern, information not previously published. If it was, its significance can only be understood as Durie weaves together the strands of a subtle mosaic, the impact of which is increasingly overlaid on unsuspecting populations and their naive or opportunistic leaders. Such is usually an exploitable weakness in decaying democracies.

Durie's subject matter is the results of past Islamic conquests. Three choices were offered to subjugated populations: convert to Islam, resist and be killed, submit and become a dhimmi.

Dhimmitude is a term that relates to the Islamic treatment of non-Muslims. A well known contemporary authority, Bat Ye'or, defines it as "the totality of the characteristics developed in the long term by communities subjected in their own homeland to the laws and ideology imported through jihad" (p.118). In this process non-Muslims lost their own distinct identity and were obliged to be indebted to and grateful for Islamic conquest.

The preliminary expression of this indebtedness was a compulsory tax [jizya] levied upon all non-Muslims for the privilege of being allowed to remain alive within an Islamic jurisdiction. Payment of this tax afforded the indulgence of "protection". But that was merely the start of the process of humiliation and subjugation.

Through objective analysis and scholarly rationality, daringly freed from the self-imposed restraints of political correctness, Durie shatters the conspiracy of silence, overwhelms ignorance and considers how Islam has operated through much of its history whenever it has succeeded militarily in achieving imperialistic objectives.

His base to achieve this is a careful examination of the Quran, the Hadith (Traditions) and the Sira—biographies of the Prophet Mohammed. These sources are authoritatively foundational for all that has transpired in Islam's fourteen centuries of existence. By using Islam's own source material, applied and amply illustrated by historical and contemporary authorities within its realm, Durie's analysis and conclusions are compelling, detailing a history of massacre, rape, looting, seizure of property and enslavement (p.157), the communal implications (p160) and current behaviour toward non-Muslims in Yemen, Palestine, Egypt, Bosnia, Pakistan, Afghanistan and other places. It also serves as a salutary corrective to the shallow political platitudes of world leaders Bush, Blair, Sarkozy, Obama, UN operatives and others.

Iranian Christians say Ayatollah Khomeini did them a great favour. He took Islam off the shelf and unwrapped its pretty packaging to expose for the world what the faith is really like. Durie goes further. With clinical precision he dissects part of Islam's body of beliefs and their applications with contemporary implications.

If as Jesus said, truth will set one free (John 8:32) we are indebted to Mark Durie for shining the torch of truth into this dark history of cultural and societal genocide. The degree to which we wisely and resolutely apply this knowledge may well determine our own futures as free or dhimmi people.

Stuart Robinson
Founding Pastor of Crossway Baptist Church

A God who Hates
Wafa Sultan, *A God who Hates* (St Martin's Press: New York, 2009) ISBN 978-0-312-53835-4

Wafa Sultan describes herself as an atheist. Her autobiographical "A God who Hates" is a witness statement concerning Islam's God, of whom she writes "I did see the influence he wielded, and in order to dispel his influence, I have to deal with him as if he exists" (p.46).

At the heart of Sultan's courageous book is a testimony concerning the treatment of women in Muslim societies. This, as she experienced it, was horrific. She tells of how her grandmother was forced to welcome her grandfather's second wife by dancing at their wedding; of harrowing insights into family sexual abuse - many instances of incest rape came to her attention when pregnancy brought the female victims into her surgery; of the murder of women who had the misfortune to fall pregnant, often at the hands of the very same male relative who had raped them; of abuse by the medical profession and employers; of sexual harassment of single women in public places - the movements of female students on a bus 'resembled those mice attempting to flee from a malicious cat' (p.29); of the oppressive system of guardianship which men exercise over women in Islam; and, perhaps most movingly of all, of the self-rejecting words she heard coming from the mouths of abused female patients.

A question that cries out from this litany of suffering is 'Why?' After many years of observation and study, Sultan came to what seemed to her to be the inescapable conclusion that all the abuses she was observing around her were due to Islam and its God.

Sultan offers this warning to the world: 'The status of women in Muslim countries is a human catastrophe that the world has ignored for centuries, and for which it is now paying a high price for ignoring.' The price, she suggests, is that oppressed and subjugated women cannot raise emotionally well and mentally healthy men. The 'invisible Muslim woman' ... is ... 'the hen who incubates the eggs of terrorism.' (p.135) Sultan's answer to the post 9/11 question 'Why do they hate us?' is 'Because Muslims hate their women, and any group who hates their women can't love anyone else.' Why do they hate their women? 'Because their God does.' (p.7)

Sultan believes that the retrograde features of the God of Islam were originally due to the harsh desert environment in which he was created by the minds of the Arabs, so many centuries ago. She contends that the harsh and fear-oriented desert mind-set is merely a primitive backwardness, which must be replaced by a more enlightened worldview. The desert God of fear and hate, she says, must be displaced. This is for her an inevitable and necessary product of human progress.

Sultan holds America up as her dreamland of freedom and human dignity, a vision of the progress which she hopes the Muslim world will enjoy. However the evil of abuse of women is not limited to Islamic societies and there is something naive about Sultan's trust in progress.

Sultan provides many references to the Koran and traditions of Muhammad, in order to make clear how Islamic teachings condition Muslim men to ill-treat Muslim women. However this book is not a reference work on Islamic law. Rather it is an intensely personal document, the diary of a soul walking a long, difficult and dangerous journey out of darkness into hard-won freedom. The author is a compassionate and brave woman, who writes with terrible frankness about her experiences, but dares to dream and hope for a better world, shaped by a loving God.

Mark Durie
Vicar, St Mark's Caulfield

The World Turned Upside Down

Melanie Phillips, *The World Turned Upside Down* (Encounter Books: New York, 2010) ISBN – 13: 978-1-59403-375-9, ISBN – 10: 1-59403-375-7.

In the West we are involved in a war of worldviews. On the one side is the Judeo-Christian worldview. Opposed to it are various contenders, chief of which are two main rivals: radical secular leftism, and radical Islam. Indeed, Phillips notes the many striking similarities between the Western progressives and the Islamists.

Both are a threat to the free West and to Judeo-Christian values because both are involved in coercive utopianism; both demonise any dissent from their ideology; and both have declared war against Israel and the Jewish people. And often these two forces find themselves working together in their assault on the Judeo-Christian West.

In this volume the incisive British journalist examines in detail these and related threats, and highlights how successful these attacks have been in the past few decades. Those familiar with her regular columns for the *Spectator* and other publications will find familiar ground here.

But this volume allows her to take her brief opinion pieces and develop them in much more depth and detail. In 18 meaty chapters she chronicles this war of worldviews, and demonstrates how very much at risk Western civilisation in fact is. She clearly delineates "The global battle over God, truth, and power" as the subtitle puts it.

She covers quite a bit of ground in this substantial volume. She offers a wide-ranging probe into the problems we face and the reasons behind them. Various confrontations with the Judeo-Christian worldview are explored in some detail. For example, she has chapters on the radical environmental movement, including the global warming crowd.

She assesses the politicisation of science and how radical agendas are being pushed in the name of science. She also notes how scientism has replaced hard science, whether among the atheistic Darwinists or the climate change true believers.

She also assesses the suicidal tendencies of the West over the past few centuries, noting how a collapse in the belief in God turned out not to be liberating as imagined, but enslaving. The rise of totalistic police states, coercive utopias, and depersonalising social engineering, has been among the bitter fruit of the attempt to sacralise man while dethroning God.

About a third of the book deals with Israel and the war against the Jews. Phillips looks at how Israel so often gets a bad press from the mainstream media, and how both the Islamists and the political left seem to have Israel in their sites.

Like all writers, she had an obvious point of reference which she proceeds from. She happens to be English, and Jewish. Thus while the Western world is discussed in general, much of her commentary focuses on the UK in particular.

And as a Jewish author, she has certain takes on other monotheistic faith systems. She calls herself "an agnostic although traditionally minded Jew". She obviously sees Islam as a clear enemy of the Jews and of Israel. With Christianity she makes more obvious distinctions.

She rightly recognises that Protestant evangelicals are "passionately supportive of Israel" while the liberal progressive churches are mainly hostile to the nation. She sees the established Church of England as especially tainted by leftist, pagan and secular nostrums and values, including contempt for Israel.

My admittedly biased Protestantism finds what may be biases on her part concerning Christianity. She can be guilty of somewhat sweeping or overloaded charges, such as: "Medieval Christianity – like contemporary Islamism – stamped out dissent by killing or conversion".

Or she can say rather sloppily, "the New Testament accuses the Jews of deicide and curses them for all time". Leaving aside some of these unfortunate and somewhat reckless remarks, one can take much from the book as a whole. Phillips has been a tireless defender of the West and its democratic freedoms, and she has been quite bold in promoting Christian freedoms.

As she notes, "Christianity is under direct and unremitting cultural assault from those who want to destroy the bedrock values of

Western civilization." She has often defended the Christian faith when so many Christians have been unwilling or unable to do so.

Indeed, her passion in this regard puts many Christians to shame. She rightly is perplexed and dismayed at the war against the West, and why so many Westerners – including Christians – are simply standing by, watching it collapse around them.

Indeed, she finishes her book by asking whether the West in fact wants to defend itself and its many important goods any longer. Or, could it be that "Western civilization has now reached a point where it has stopped trying to survive"?

That is certainly the question of the hour. Do we have the will to resist, or have we already raised the white flag of surrender? Phillips has done her part in sounding the alarm, detailing the war we are in, and highlighting the many battlefronts this war is waging on.

She has done her service admirably. It is hoped that readers of this important book will now do theirs.

Bill Muehlenberg
CultureWatch (http://www.billmuehlenberg.com/)

Interrupting Ehrman: another attack on the reliability of the Bible

Bart Ehrman, *Jesus Interrupted: Revealing the hidden contradictions in the Bible (and why we don't know about them)* (Harper Collins: New York, 2009, 292 pp). ISBN 978-0-06-117393-6.

In a previous article in *Evangelicals Now* I reviewed several books by Bart Ehrman.

I observed that Ehrman had previously been a professing evangelical, but thereafter became an agnostic with a strongly liberal agenda in regard to biblical criticism. Ehrman is a prolific writer, gifted to present his work in a very accessible way for readers who have little academic theological education. The problem for evangelicals is that this means he is popularising often hardened modernist biblical criticism. This latest book has already received considerable attention in America.

Ammunition for Islam

A further problem, as my previous review mentioned, is that Ehrman's works are utilised by Islamic polemicists in their attacks upon the Bible, as demonstrated by a cursory glance at Muslim polemical literature and websites. Indeed, his books are on sale in Islamic bookshops. Recently, at a meeting between evangelicals and Muslims, one Muslim in the audience referred to his writings in order to suggest that the biblical text was untrustworthy. It follows that in order to safeguard untrained members of our congregations, we must be aware of the challenge that his writings present and be able to respond to them — because sooner or later ordinary people in the pew are going to approach their pastors with reports that Islamic missionaries have attempted to shake their faith with Ehrman's material.

Ehrman's new book once again shows that he is an impressive communicator, able to take often difficult and intricate issues and present them in an accessible and readable fashion for 'the common man'. In that sense, his defection to agnosticism and theological liberalism is a tragic loss to evangelicalism. Would that more evangelical scholars were possessed of his communication gifts! However, it must be immediately objected that it is most unlikely that any such scholar would be able to interest a major publishing firm to take on a work defending the Bible. The reason? There would be limited demand for it. The ordinary public has a craving for 'scandal stories' about 'the church', especially tales that involve 'conspiracies' — note the popularity of *The Da Vinci Code*. Even the sub-title of Ehrman's book hints at this — why indeed does the general public not know about 'contradictions' in the Bible — indeed, why are they 'hidden' (and by whom)?

Nothing new

It must first be observed that there really is nothing new in Ehrman's book; the points he raises have been made — and addressed — many times before. He acknowledges this on p.2: 'The perspectives that I present in the following chapters are not my own idiosyncratic views of the Bible. They are the views that have held sway for many, many years among the majority of serious critical scholars teaching in the universities and seminaries of North America and Europe...' He repeats this point towards the end of the book (p.271). There he tells us that the 'views' to which he refers are inspired by 'the historical-critical approach to the New Testament...' The outcome of liberal presuppositions when attached to this system becomes clear: one cannot speak of the underlying unity of the New Testament, because this is the product of reading the Gospels 'vertically' (p.21), 'from beginning to end', i.e. from Matthew to John, whereas they should be read 'horizontally' — essentially, comparing the same story in the different Gospels, which he claims reveals various 'differences and discrepancies'.

Presuppositions

Because of the constraints of space, it is impossible in this article to address all the examples Ehrman quotes, but they have been addressed many times before — e.g. the purported differences between the cleansing of the Temple in Mark and John. Craig Blomberg's excellent book *The Historical Reliability of the Gospels* can be recommended in this regard. Our point here is that Ehrman allows his liberal presuppositions to influence his treatment of the subject. His tone is somewhat condescending when he suggests that if one is 'creative enough' one could 'figure out a plausible explanation for both accounts being right' (p.22). This merely shows that Ehrman is determined to see the accounts as impossibly divergent, rather than to consider alternative proposals.

Ehrman makes similar points about the date of the Last Supper in relation to the Day of Preparation in Mark and John for Passover, the Baptism of Jesus, the death of Judas, the Resurrection accounts, etc. Again, there is nothing new here, and all these points have been answered many times. One problem with Ehrman's book — which probably would face any book of this nature — is that, in order to make issues accessible for the ordinary reader, the detailed examination that such points deserve is sacrificed. Indeed, to answer all of Ehrman's points in detail would probably require several volumes!

Sometimes Ehrman's non-believing presuppositions come through in his treatment of biblical material, e.g. his scepticism about the Star of Bethlehem. He wonders what kind of star could move 'slowly enough for the wise men to follow on foot or on camel, stops, starts again, and stops again?' (p.52), and then asks: 'And how exactly does a star stop over a house? I tell my students to go outside on some starry night, pick one of the brightest stars in the sky, and figure out which house on their block it is standing over'. He acknowledges that the narrative describes 'a miraculous event', but wonders what kind of astronomical body the writer has in mind. Surely, the point is, we are not dealing with natural, but rather supernatural phenomena, so there is inevitably a measure of mystery that human finite scientific analysis cannot penetrate?

Anonymous Gospels?

At other points, Ehrman seems to have sacrificed scholarly discussion for either brevity or polemic. Note his claim that the Gospels are 'anonymous' (p.102ff). Surely some reference to the writings of Hengel and Bauckham at this point would have been in order. In the latter's *Jesus and the Eyewitnesses* (p.300ff), he notes that, in classical times, many ancient biographies were of the same structure as the Gospels in this regard, and that the initial circulation of such works would have been among 'friends or acquaintances of the author who would know who the author was from the oral context in which the work was first read'. Given the evidence for the wide circulation of the Gospels among the first-century churches, it follows that the recipients were, indeed, aware of their authorship.

Indeed, Bruce Metzger, a lecturer at the very same Princeton Theological Seminary where Ehrman first moved away from evangelicalism, observed in his book *The Canon of the New Testament* (pp.301-302), 'In the book trade of antiquity the title of a roll that contained a single work would have its title written on a strip or tag ... of papyrus or vellum projecting from the back of the roll. Inside the roll the title was placed also at the end of the work. Usually the title is expressed in the simplest possible form: the author's name in the genitive case, then the title, followed (if applicable) by the number of the book'. Yet Ehrman never addresses this point.

Moreover, what can we say about his assertion about the linguistic knowledge of Jesus and the Apostles (p.105ff): 'As Galilean Jews, Jesus's followers, like Jesus himself, would have been speakers of Aramaic. As rural folk they probably would not have any knowledge of Greek; if they did, it would have been extremely rough...' Surely Hengel demonstrated long ago that Palestine had been extensively Hellenised as a consequence of Alexander the Great, and there is evidence of Jewish gravestones in Jerusalem with Greek inscriptions, to say nothing of the fact that Simon bar Cochba was known to write in Greek. Galilee, bordering Gentile areas and with Greek-speaking cities adjacent, would have been especially open to dual use of Greek and Aramaic. In many societies bi-lingualism is the norm rather the exception, whatever the social standing of the populace.

Motives

What is Ehrman's motive in writing this book? He tells us that it is 'to make serious scholarship on the Bible and earliest Christianity accessible and available' to ordinary people (p.271). The problem is that the only 'serious scholarship' he makes accessible is of a decidedly liberal bent, with essentially little acknowledgement of 'serious' conservative scholars and their works. Another goal seems to be to encourage pastors to convey the 'historical-critical method' (as he sees it) in their 'adult education classes' (note the US-reference therein) (p.272, cf. pp.12-16).

In a paradoxical way, Ehrman has a point here. As he observes, Sunday preaching is necessarily 'devotional', but, even in Britain, there are opportunities for theological instruction during the week. Generations of Scots, Welsh, Ulstermen, and English 'Dissenters' were raised on the Shorter Catechism (and their Baptist/Independent variants), and Richard Baxter was famous for catechising his parishioners. Available resources exist for instructing church members in conservative scholarship on biblical canonicity, text, elements of early church history, etc.

Age of popular smears

The problem is not just that pastors are unwilling or unable to put them in place, as Ehrman thinks, but also that attendance at such events would probably be limited. Yet, living as we do in an age of popular smears against Christ and the Bible, such as *The Da Vinci Code*, and in many parts of Britain facing the challenge of Muslim mission which utilises the works of Ehrman and others to unsettle ordinary church members, such meetings are no luxury. Both 'pulpit and pew' must start to take the issue of general theological/historical education more seriously, if we are not to lose another generation to unbelief. Ehrman's own tragic descent into agnosticism is surely a warning of this.

Dr. Anthony McRoy
This review first appeared in the November 2009 issue of *Evangelicals Now* (www.e-n.org.au).

CSIOF News and Activities

CSIOF Courses and Thesis Supervision

The Centre continues to offer a range of general and specialist subjects to BCV students and the Church community. In 2010, the CSIOF Faculty taught postgraduate units on *Islam: History and Institutions*, *Christian Ministry in Islamic Contexts*, and *Reading Arabic Texts Extension*. *Living Faiths* was also taught at undergraduate/graduate level, and *World Religions* at Certificate level. Two community courses were held in Melbourne's CBD on *Christian Apologetics to Islam*, and *Understanding the Qur'an from a Christian Perspective*.

CSIOF Faculty also currently supervise four ThD student theses and three MA student projects, on areas relating to Islam.

CSIOF Faculty, Out and About

On top of the central supervision and teaching activities of the CSIOF, the CSIOF faculty remain active in their involvement in national and international conferences, mission trips, varied speaking engagements and activities, and in the publication of a range of articles on contemporary issues facing the Church today.

Dr Peter Riddell, Dean of the CSIOF, has been involved in a number of international teaching and speaking engagements. During a trip to Europe he presented at Oxford Centre for Mission Studies, the London Institute for Contemporary Christianity, and at a Benedictine Monastery in northern France. He also took part in an interview on UK's "Revelation TV", and spoke at a mission conference in Germany run by Eusebia Mission Agency. Closer to home, as guest lecturer, Peter took postgraduate intensives on *Islam in the Modern World* at Laidlaw College in New Zealand, and on *Engaging Islam* at Moore College in Sydney. Drawing on previous experience in the aid and development sector, Peter addressed the topic of *"Development by Muslims, among Muslims and with Muslims's Prospects and Challenges*, at a World Vision Staff Theological Forum in Melbourne, and also presented a paper on an early Malay Islamic manuscript at a seminar for Monash University's Centre for South East Asian Studies. Peter spoke on *The Call to Islam: Diverse Methods and Varied Responses*, at the CMS Victoria "Summer under the Son" conference, and on *Understanding Muslims* at their July Day Conference. He also responded to an invitation of the BCV Alumni in Queensland to conduct a series of seminars in Brisbane, chaired a Mission Network Lunch at BCV, and was involved in a number of other local and interstate speaking engagements.

Bernie Power, CSIOF Lecturer, has also been involved in a number of international and national activities. He took a group to Sudan over the summer break, teaching English at an Islamic University, and was also a part of the AFFWAN (YWAM) outreach on the Gold Coast earlier this year. During a visit to Cairo, Bernie presented at the E2S conference in Cairo, Egypt, and at an Evangelistic Storytelling conference, and while in New Zealand, spoke at Laidlaw College, Faith Bible College, and Interserve's National Conference in Auckland. Bernie also gave a series of presentations at the MACH Conference in Sydney on grace-filled responses to our Muslim neighbours, and along with Peter, spoke at the IGWA2010 Interserve Conference in Melbourne. He continues to frequently speak at local churches across Melbourne, on issues relating to Christian-Muslim relations, including "The Future of Islam in Australia" at a recent MCD Conference, and is involved in a regular meeting of international students at La Trobe University.

CSIOF Faculty Publications

Over the last twelve months, the CSIOF Faculty have published journalism articles in *Church Times, Evangelicals Now, Touchstone Magazine, Kairos Journal, The Melbourne Anglican, Victorian Baptist Witness, Eternity*, and Interserve's *Go!* Magazine.

They have also published other various works, including the following by Peter Riddell:

"Exegesis" & "Tunku Abdul Rahman", in John Esposito (ed.), *Oxford Encyclopedia of the Islamic World*, New York: Oxford University Press, 2009.

"A film window into political struggle in Malaysia", *Indonesia and the Malay World* 37/109 (November 2009), 373-376.

"Shari'ah-Mindedness in the Malay World and the Indian Connection: The Contribution of Nur al-Din al-Raniri and Nik Abdul Aziz bin Haji Nik Mat", in Feener, R. Michael & Sevea, Terenjit (eds), *Islamic Connections: Studies of South and Southeast Asia*, Singapore: Institute for Southeast Asian Studies, 2009, 175-94.

CSIOF Students

On 4 August, two of CSIOF's ThD students were involved in an Islamic Studies Inter-Institutional Higher Degree Research Forum, at the Australian Catholic University (ACU). This day was an opportunity for research students from the CSIOF, ACU and Monash University, whose research focus is on Islam, to share aspects of their research in closed session. The papers presented at this forum included *Becoming a da'iyya, Muslim scholars respond to the Hadith,* and *The concept of jihad in pre-Islamic Syrian Christian writings.*

CSIOF ThD students also took a number of sessions at the MACH Conference in Sydney.

Postgraduate Research Seminars on Islam and Related Topics 2010

The Prayers and Parables of Muhammad
Bernie Power, 23 March

The Theology of Islamic Anti-semitism
Mark Durie, 23 March

The 7 Sleepers of Ephesus: Christian and Islamic Accounts.
Dr. Mehmet Akif Koç, Ankara University, Turkey, 17 August

Muslim Women's Gatherings and Leadership
ThD student, 17 August

Information & Support Form

Name:	_____
Address:	_____
Phone: _____	Email: _____

Would you like to stay informed?

- ☐ Please add my name to the CSIOF mailing list
- ☐ I would like to regularly receive the CSIOF Bulletin
- ☐ I would like to regularly receive the CSIOF Occasional Papers
- ☐ Please send me information regarding CSIOF programs.
- ☐ Please send me information on courses at BCV.

Would you like to financially support the work of the CSIOF?

Please specify amount: $_____

- ☐ Cheque (made payable to the Bible College of Victoria)
- ☐ Credit Card: Expiry date: ___/___
  ☐ Visa ☐ Mastercard
  Card No.
  ____ ____ ____ ____
  Name on card:_____
- ☐ Other:_____

All donations to the CSIOF are tax deductible

Please return this form to:
Centre for the Study of Islam and Other Faiths

www.ingramcontent.com/pod-product-compliance
Lightning Source LLC
Chambersburg PA
CBHW051456290426
44109CB00016B/1782